inside pitching

inside pitching

ferguson jenkins

with
dave fisher

Contemporary Books, Inc.
Chicago

Published by Contemporary Books, Inc.
180 North Michigan Avenue, Chicago, Illinois 60601
Manufactured in the United States of America
Library of Congress Catalog Card Number: 79-64997
International Standard Book Number: 0-8092-8847-8 (cloth)
           0-8092-8845-1 (paper)

Published simultaneously in Canada by
Beaverbooks
953 Dillingham Road
Pickering, Ontario L1W 1Z7
Canada

preface

I don't remember the first time I held a baseball, but it must have been a wonderful experience because I grew up loving the game. When I was growing up in Canada, I played all sports and was proficient in almost everything I tried, but there always was something special about baseball. In my early days I was an outfielder like my dad; then I became a first baseman and, finally, a pitcher.

The pitcher is the most important player on the field. There are no hard and accurate statistics proving how important a pitcher is to a baseball team, but it is worth noting that fully one-third of all major league baseball players are pitchers.

The first time I stepped onto the pitcher's mound I felt awkward and out of place. I knew what I wanted to do, but my body wouldn't cooperate. So I worked at it, and pitching eventually became a natural movement for my body. I could throw hard, and I had control, but I didn't really begin to learn what pitching was all about until I entered professional baseball.

Pitching is not easy. I have heard people say that hitting a baseball is the toughest thing to do in all sports, but I wonder if pitching the ball isn't tougher. It is not the movement of pitching that is difficult—the basic movement is relatively easy—but the planning and execution that goes into every pitch. A pitcher must be able to know what the hitter and base runner are thinking; he must be fully aware of the game situation, and on the basis of all his calculations he must throw the ball 60 feet and 6 inches to a specific spot without letting the batter hit it.

There are no shortcuts to becoming a good pitcher. You must have a thorough understanding of the game (including all the rules); you must practice constantly and keep yourself in good physical condition; and you must play hard and play to win. In this book I've tried to explain some of the things it has taken me years to learn. I've explained pitching techniques as I know them and use them today. I have not concentrated on the rules except where they can be used in planning strategy, because regulations can be learned easily from any baseball rule book. I have emphasized those special tips and techniques that you can apply to your pitching to help you develop a unique pitching style.

As you read this book, you will notice that special terms appear in italics the first time they are mentioned. The complete definitions for these terms appear in the glossary at the back of the book.

With the information you learn from this book in your head you will *know* what it takes to be a better pitcher. But simply knowing how to be better is only half of what it takes to *be* a good pitcher. You must practice—I can't stress that enough.

contents

PITCHING IS MORE THAN . . . just getting out on the mound, throwing the ball 60'6″, and hoping the batter doesn't drive it over the fence. To be a good pitcher you must back up your physical skills with mental know-how and practice constantly.

chapter 1

BEFORE STEPPING ON THE MOUND

When I was a boy, baseball was not my national game. I grew up in Chatham, Ontario, a Canadian city about an hour's drive north of Detroit. Like most Canadian youngsters I played a lot of hockey, and I was good enough to reach the Junior B Division, which is only two steps away from the National Hockey League. But as soon as the snow melted, in April or May, I was a devoted baseball player. My dad had been a semipro player, and he passed his love for baseball on to me. Whenever he had the time, he would take me out to the park to play. I was pretty tall even then, and he would take one look at my lanky legs and say, "Left field, Son. Go out to left field." For hours he would hit long *flies* and hard *grounders,* and I would run to catch the ball.

By the time I was 13 I was 6′ 1″ and still growing. I was playing Bantam League ball, and I became a first baseman when my manager said, "Put the tall, skinny kid on first base." It wasn't until I was 16 that I threw my first pitch in an organized game. The pitcher on our team came up with a sore arm, and I volunteered to pitch for him. I didn't even know how to wind up. I just took the ball and threw it as hard as I could. It worked out all right: I pitched six *innings* of no-hit baseball. From that day on I considered myself a pitcher, although I didn't really begin to learn how to pitch until I was 19.

Being an *outfielder* my dad could not teach me very much about pitching, but one thing he did emphasize was the importance of using the proper equipment. Baseball equipment isn't of a protective nature because baseball isn't a contact sport. But you can be badly hurt if you use the wrong equipment—not only physically but in your ability to play.

BALL

The rule books describe a baseball as "a sphere formed by yarn wound around a small core of cork, rubber, or similiar material, covered with two strips of white horsehide tightly stitched together 9 to 9¼ inches in circumference." I never get that technical in describing the ball. What concerns me is that the baseball is the only weapon I have when I'm up against another team.

Every baseball has a different "feel" to it, whether it's a major league baseball handmade in Haiti or a machine-made ball. The seams could be high; the ball could be wound too tightly, or the cover could be a little slippery, but in some way every baseball has its own distinct feel. When I'm pitching, I examine very carefully each baseball that I'm going to use. I hold it loosely in my fingers until it feels comfortable. Never throw a baseball that doesn't feel completely comfortable, because if you're thinking about some peculiarity of the ball, you're not thinking about the hitter. He has enough advantages without your failing to concentrate.

When I was a boy, I thought nothing of playing with a wet or soggy ball. But I've learned since that it's not a good idea for a pitcher to throw a wet ball, because it gets very heavy and puts an extra strain on his arm.

Some pitchers like to "doctor" the ball so that it feels more comfortable. For example, Whitey Ford used to let his catcher put a nick in the ball he was to pitch. Don Drysdale would "load it up," or spit on the ball. Many pitchers like to throw a ball that is particularly dirty. I don't do any of those things, and I don't recommend them. Unless you know exactly what a nick, a dark spot, or moisture will make a ball do, it doesn't make any sense to throw a doctored ball. The idea is to make the ball go where you want it to go, and doing anything to the surface of the ball might prevent that.

PITCHER'S MOUND

A few years ago the Baseball Rules Committee decided to give hitters an advantage by lowering the height of the *pitcher's mound*. This was done to encourage more action in the game, but we pitchers needed that about as much as we needed Henry Aaron coming to bat with the bases loaded. The higher the pitcher's mound is, the easier it is to pitch. You get more power coming down off a high mound than you do by throwing from an almost level position. But there's nothing you can do about the height of a mound except get used to it. With a little luck it will be your home for several hours, and you'll be doing yourself a favor by being a good housekeeper.

Before you throw your first pitch, make a careful inspection tour. Walk off the back of the mound a couple of times just to get the feel of it in case you have to get off quickly during a game. I've seen more than one pitcher fall head over heels trying to field a bouncer hit behind him, because he didn't realize how steep the drop off the mound was. Once you've given the mound a general inspection, comb the area for stones that may distract you or cause the ball to take a bad hop. Then throw a few easy pitches to see if you're striding into a hole. If you are, fill it up. Also, if the opposing pitcher has done some excavation just in front of the *pitching rubber* that feels uncomfortable, repair that damage, too. If it has been raining and the mound is muddy, try to build a dry spot to stride into. This dry spot will prevent you from slipping once you have released the ball. In some of the ball parks in which I've played I've had to do so much construction work before I was ready to pitch that I thought I should be wearing a hard hat rather than a baseball cap.

RESIN BAG

The *resin bag* is used to dry perspiration from your hands. Using the resin bag helps you to get a better grip on the ball, preventing the ball from slipping out of your hand too soon. If you perspire a great deal, the resin bag is a handy little thing to carry in your back pocket. But it also can be used for other things. Sometimes when I'm being hit pretty well and I'm having trouble concentrating, I walk off the mound and pick up the resin bag. I just hold it in my hand and stare at it for a minute. It really helps me to get my concentration back.

The resin bag also can be used for signals. The Chicago Cubs use many different sets of catcher's signals, depending on the situation. The resin bag is used as the indicator. If it's lying on the first base side of the mound, it means we're using one set of signals. If it's behind the mound, out of the catcher's sight, it indicates a second set. And if it's on the third base side, indicating we've gone through the first two sets of signals, it means Fergie is in trouble and please have the hot water running in the showers.

PITCHING RUBBER

When I was playing ball in Canada, we kids would nail a piece of an old tire into the ground and call it a pitching rubber. That piece of old tire worked just as well as the white rubber at Wrigley Field, which measures 24 inches long by 6 inches wide. Before you throw your first pitch, check to make sure that the rubber is stable and secured firmly into the ground. It should not move at all when you push off of it. If it does, it will not only cause you to lose power in your pitches, but it also can cause a severe muscle strain in your arm.

I recommend that everyone pitch from the spot on the rubber where he feels most comfortable. I personally prefer to pitch from the middle of the rubber, but that doesn't mean I always pitch from that spot.

For example, against the Dodgers, who put a lot of left-handed hitters in their lineup when I pitch against them, I move to the left side of the rubber. If a team overloads its lineup with righties, which they don't usually do because I'm a right-handed pitcher, I move to the right side of the rubber. But once you've chosen the spot on the rubber from which you want to pitch on a certain day, it is not a good idea to move around too much — it prevents you from getting into a regular routine.

GLOVE

I can still remember having what I thought was my first real baseball glove, one of my dad's old ones from his equipment bag. He had cut the center out of the pocket to give him better glove control, but every time I caught a ball with it, I thought I had broken my hand. However, I did learn one thing from that glove — the importance of having a glove that fits properly.

Buying a glove is a substantial investment; you should take your time and choose it carefully (Diagram 1). Your glove should be big enough to give your

DIAGRAM 1. The glove.

fingers plenty of room to move around but not so big that you don't have full control with one hand. As you grow older, you naturally will need a bigger and heavier glove, but it's not a good idea to buy a glove "to grow into." On the other hand, a glove shouldn't be so small that it cramps your fingers. I started using a six-finger model when I was with the Arkansas Travellers in the minor leagues, and I haven't changed yet.

Never buy a glove just because it's the same model that a player you admire uses. Buy a Ferguson Jenkins model, for example, only if it's the glove that feels most comfortable to you. For most of 1971 I used a Juan Marichal model because that was the glove that felt the best.

Some of the players are beginning to use different colored gloves. Vida Blue used a blue glove for a while. I see nothing wrong with colored gloves; I own a blue model myself. The all-important requirement about a glove is that it must fit your hand properly.

A good glove can be rather expensive, so you should always take good care of it. Going over it with saddle soap softens the leather and prevents it from cracking. If your glove gets wet, dry it off with a towel. Don't put it near a heater; let it dry naturally. When you put your glove away for the winter, it's a good idea to leave a baseball wrapped in the pocket. It helps the glove to keep its shape.

UNIFORM

Many youngsters are concerned more with how they look in a baseball uniform than how that uniform should be worn properly. They are making a big mistake. A baseball uniform consists of many individual pieces of functional equipment. It is not a costume; every piece of clothing is worn for a specific reason. Being properly outfitted

is as important to your well-being as it is to your performance on the field. When I was growing up, I certainly didn't have an expensive baseball uniform with the name of some team written across the front — not many young players do. A baseball jersey is nothing more than a glorified sweat shirt, and sliding pads can be compared to thick, durable bermuda shorts. If you don't have some of the following equipment, don't worry about it — substitute something that is just as functional as the kind used by the pros.

Jersey, Pants, Socks

I remember the first time I put on a major league uniform. It said "Phillies" across the front of the jersey, and I sat there and traced the felt lettering with my fingertips. Then I stood in front of a mirror and made sure that uniform looked perfect. But I've learned better since then; it doesn't really matter what a uniform looks like as long as it is comfortable. Today many players have their uniforms tapered. I certainly won't argue the fact that they look great standing on the field. But I just don't think that the way a uniform looks is that important. What is important, especially for a pitcher, is that you have total freedom of movement. A pitcher does more moving of his legs and shoulders than anyone on the field, and if a uniform is the slightest bit restrictive, it really can hurt his performance.

I think that the jersey, sometimes called the uniform jacket, should give you plenty of shoulder movement but should not bunch up in the chest. Some players stick their jersey inside the band of their athletic supporter so that the jersey won't come out of their pants. The pants should be loose enough so that you can kick your leg as high as you like without feeling restricted, but they should not be so loose that they

YOUR UNIFORM . . . should fit you properly, which means that you should be so comfortable wearing it that you are not conscious of socks slipping, legs binding, or spikes pinching when you are out on the mound.

balloon when a breeze comes up.

As far as socks go, whether you wear a pair of knee-high sanitary socks with the uniform stirrup socks over them or one or two pairs of sweat socks, just make sure the elastic around the top is taut. There is nothing as bothersome as a sock that keeps falling down throughout the game.

Under the Uniform

I guess you might say I'm a bit of a fanatic when it comes to keeping my arm warm. In fact, during the first two years that I played professional baseball, I slept with a sweat shirt on. I think every pitcher has to decide for himself what he feels comfortable wearing. I wear quite a bit of underclothing, and another pitcher might feel restricted wearing as much. But remember, I grew up in Canada, and I got used to wearing a lot of clothing to protect me against the cold.

The first thing I put on every day, whether I'm scheduled to pitch or not, is a lightweight T-shirt with the sleeves cut off. Any type of cotton shirt will absorb a great amount of perspiration and keep your uniform from getting soggy and heavy. I cut off the sleeves to give my arms the greatest amount of freedom. Next comes my long underwear, top and bottom, which also picks up some perspiration and helps to retain my body heat. I try to keep my arm protected whether it's freezing cold or boiling hot on the field. On top of the long underwear I put on the uniform undershirt — the shirt with colored sleeves that protrude from the uniform jersey, which is worn over the undershirt. Although the Cubs issue both long- and short-sleeved undershirts, I always wear the long sleeves to keep that arm warm.

I don't wear a wool dickey or turtleneck because wool irritates my skin. Many players do, however, and they say that they feel fine with them on; it's your decision. Finally, the sanitary socks go on. These are much lighter than regular sweat socks, and they don't weigh your feet down with perspiration, but sweat socks will serve the same purpose of keeping your feet clean and dry. It's not a bad idea to wear a couple pairs of sweat socks to prevent blisters when you're breaking in a new pair of *spikes*. Never put on a dirty or soggy pair of socks.

As far as I'm concerned, the athletic supporter and fiber glass *cup* are the baseball player's two most important pieces of protective equipment. I never step out on a baseball field without them, even if I'm just going to run in the outfield. The athletic supporter provides protection against strain, and the cup, which fits in a pocket provided for it in the athletic supporter, protects you from being badly hurt by a pitched or thrown ball. Sometimes I'll buy a cup a little smaller than I normally would wear because a cup of the correct size has a tendency to rub along the sides of my legs and irritate them. I put the cup and athletic supporter on under my long underwear. Probably the most important thing to remember about your athletic supporter is to always make sure that it is clean before putting it on to prevent irritation.

Years ago almost every baseball player wore sliding pads; if you've ever seen a picture of the rock-covered infields of those days, you understand why. Today there are still players who wear sliding pads. Others, however, wear bermuda shorts under their uniforms. My long underwear serves the same purpose as sliding pads, preventing me from getting leg burns when I slide.

Pitching Jacket

Before I signed my first professional contract, a baseball scout gave me a very important bit of advice. He saw me walking around without a jacket and bawled me out. "Remember," he said finally, "you've got to protect your business interest." Always wear a pitching jacket on the days you're throwing, even if it's 95° outside. When you're pitching, you're putting a great deal of strain on your arm, and it's very important never to let your arm cool down. I've never had a sore arm in my professional baseball career because I've taken all the precautions. Not only do I wear the nylon jacket, but when I'm in the *dugout,* I put on a heavily insulated wool jacket.

Spikes

The Cubs wear two different types of baseball shoes, one for artificial fields and another for natural grass. Since you probably won't play on artificial turf for a while, you probably will need only one pair of spikes. If your league allows metal *cleats,* I recommend you get them. However, rubber cleats also provide good traction.

Buying spikes is just a bit different than buying regular shoes. If you've decided to get regular leather spikes, get them a half size smaller than your normal shoe size; if you're getting the lightweight kangaroo spikes, get them a size to a size and a half smaller than you would wear normally. In both cases the kangaroo and calf leather will stretch to fit your foot, and you will have a form-fitting baseball shoe.

Pitchers usually wear out their spikes faster than any other player because they constantly are scraping the edges of the spikes along the ground. I go through a pair about every two months, but since you're not pitching every fourth day, yours should last considerably longer. Before you start pitching in your shoes, you should do quite a bit of running to break them in. You also should have a toeplate put on the area that you scrape along the mound. You can determine the area of your spikes that is going to get the most wear after pitching a few times. Any local shoemaker can put a toeplate on for you. And while you're having that done, you should have *mud guards* put on the bottoms of the shoes.

After each time you've finished playing, make sure that your shoes are dry and that you have cleaned off as much mud and dirt as possible.

I don't think it's a good idea to pitch in sneakers. Sneakers are fine for outfielders, but a pitcher needs the kind of traction to push off the rubber that sneakers cannot provide.

Headgear

Your baseball cap should sit comfortably and securely on top of your head. Many young pitchers fold the brow of their caps into a crown because they feel it looks better, but this folded cap easily can slide down or fall off while you're pitching. Let the outfielders play with their caps — it gives them something to do all day. When selecting your cap, if you have a choice, get one with a sweatband in it.

I don't wear glasses, but I was with the Phillies when they had a relief pitcher named Ryne Duren. He had the thickest glasses you've ever seen, and he used them as a weapon. On coming in from the *bullpen,* the first thing he would do on the mound was take his glasses off. Even the batter could see they were thicker than a soda bottle. He'd wipe them off a couple of times, and then he'd peer in, actually squint in, and take the catcher's sign. Ryne then would let loose with a tremendous *fast ball* that would go about 15 feet over the catcher's head. Not too many batters ever dug in on Ryne Duren.

Glasses are no problem to a pitcher, and many great ones have worn them; others prefer to wear contact lenses. I have three suggestions to make as far as glasses are concerned. First, if you don't see well (sometimes I have problems at night), have your catcher put white tape on his fingertips—it will help you to pick up his signals. Second, always carry a handkerchief in your back pocket to wipe your glasses in case they fog over. Third, make sure you have an elastic band attached to the temples of your glasses and brought around the back of your head to keep the glasses from sliding while you're pitching.

BAT

Your job as a pitcher is to keep the bat from hitting the ball — except when you're up at bat. A pitcher who can hit the ball will keep himself from being removed from

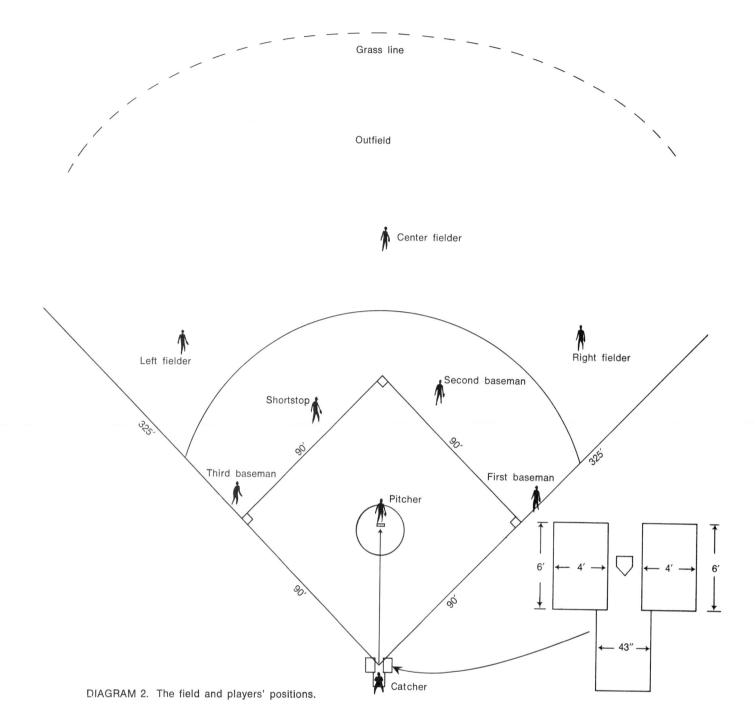

DIAGRAM 2. The field and players' positions.

many tight ball games. The most important thing in choosing a bat is to pick out one that you can handle easily. If you are going up to bat in a bunting situation, use a bat with more "meat" on the thick end. A thicker bat gives you a wider bunting area on the surface.

PLAYING FIELD

If you've ever seen the Chicago Cubs play on television, you've probably heard the announcer refer to "the friendly confines of Wrigley Field." Any player who has ever pitched there will tell you that those confines are not in the slightest bit friendly. Wrigley Field leads the majors in total home runs hit every year, but like any other ball park, it has its advantages. For example, if I get in a jam, I can easily turn around and get some advice from my center fielder.

Before a game begins, you should carefully examine the playing field (Diagram 2). The distance between the bases is 90 feet. The bases are marked by white 15-inch-square canvas bags, which are filled with any soft material. The base bags must be between three and five inches thick and must be attached to the ground. These specifications for the field are defined completely in the baseball rule book. You might not have regulation base bags when you play, but remember, whatever you use make sure that it is safe and won't harm the runner when he slides into the base.

All major league parks built after 1958 are at least 325 feet down the foul lines, but most of the fields you'll be playing on are not that big. If the field is built around an obstruction—a school, for example—remember where the short home run distances are and pitch accordingly. Never pitch a right-handed hitter inside, for example, if it's only 240 feet down the left-field line, because he'll hit a pop-up out of the park on you. You should know how much room you have to back up the catcher and the basemen, where the dugouts or any holes in the field are, if the walls are padded, and how hard the infield is. Many parks with slow teams have the infield foul lines on an incline with the high point on fair and low point on foul so that bunts will roll foul. Others have just the opposite situation. It's important to know which kind of field you're playing on, especially when someone bunts in the eighth inning of a close game and you don't know whether to play the ball or hope that it rolls foul.

A small park such as Wrigley Field does have one important advantage for a pitcher: it forces you to concentrate on every pitch you make.

RULE BOOK

Before you can play good baseball, you have to know how to play correctly. The baseball rule book is thick and very precise, and a smart ballplayer will take full advantage of the information inside it. A quick-thinking manager or player who knows the rules has often meant the difference between winning and losing a game.

My favorite story about a ballplayer who knew the rules concerns an old-timer named Germany Schaefer, who actually stole first base from second. Schaefer was on second base, and the possible winning run was safely on third. Trying to draw a throw from the catcher, Schaefer, who knew there was no rule against running the bases backward, took off toward first. The catcher was too startled to throw, and Germany Schaefer safely reached first base. On the next pitch he took off for second again, drew a throw, and enabled the player on third to slide safely home.

Most sporting goods stores carry baseball rule books. The basic rules in the little leagues are the same as in the majors. But there are some minor differences, so to be perfectly safe, get the official rule book of the league you are playing in. Read the rules carefully; know them inside and out — knowing the rules will make a big difference in the kind of pitcher you will be.

THE STRIDE YOU TAKE . . . just before releasing the ball is a very important part of your power source, but don't try to take such a big stride that you end up being off balance, because you will ruin your follow-through and destroy your pitch.

chapter 2
THROWING A PITCH

When you are standing on the pitcher's mound with the ball in your hand, you are in command. Nothing can happen until you decide that you're ready. At this point, believe it or not, you're even more important than a television commercial — it can stop the game, but only you can start it. Getting ready to throw is a mental and physical process. You have to feel and think right. It makes no sense to throw the pitch if you think the batter is going to hit it. I like to compare the pitcher's concentration before throwing the ball to the pole vaulter's concentration before approaching the crossbar. The pole vaulter stands on his approach and mentally reviews every motion he's going to make. The pitcher does exactly the same thing except that he goes through this mental process as many as 120 times during a game.

Before you swing your hands back into your *windup,* you should be totally confident that you know which pitch you are going to throw. You should know what the strategic situation is, where your fielders are positioned, and what the batter is expecting. You should be physically comfortable and relaxed. The ball should rest easily in your glove. When all these circumstances come together in your mind, a green light will signal you to deliver the ball. At that moment you will be ready to begin your pitching motion.

STANCE

There's not too much you can do wrong when you're standing on the pitcher's mound receiving the *catcher's signal.* You should have one or both feet on the rubber, whichever feels right (Diagram 3). You should establish a stable base, which allows you to feel perfectly balanced. There's no reason to rock back and forth out there, as I have seen some young pitchers do. Keep your eyes on the target at all times.

The most important thing to remember about your stance is that it should be comfortable and consistent. After you have decided on a basic stance, you should not change it during a ball game or even a

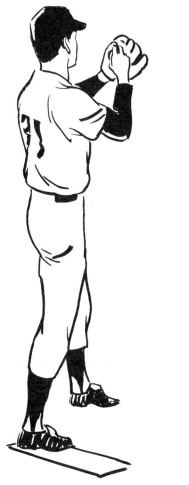

DIAGRAM 3. Stance on the rubber.

season. If you alter your stance, you're only letting yourself in for serious control problems.

HIDING THE BALL

Next to pitchers, hitters are the smartest baseball players on a team. While you're standing out there thinking about what you're going to do to them, they're concentrating on what they can do to you. Don't help them! It is extremely important that you do not tip off the pitch you're about to throw. You're not a charitable organization, and you don't have to give away any information to the hitter. Hide the baseball. When you're on the mound, the ball should be held in your glove in precisely the same place every time. However, the *laces* should be turned the proper way

for the pitch you are about to make, so that when your hand reaches for the ball, you can pick it up and throw without having to turn it for the pitch in front of the hitter. Many pitchers make the mistake of gripping their fast ball one way, the *curve* another, and the *slider* a third. Hitters will pick up on this. For example, they'll notice that you're showing more white when you're throwing the slider or no white at all when you're throwing a fast ball. Ken Holtzman was one of the worst offenders for tipping his pitch. Every time he was going to throw a curve ball, he'd wipe his hand off on his uniform. It was an unconscious habit that he had developed when he was young, but he may as well have sent the batter a telegram. Most of the hitters you'll be playing against probably won't pick up on these signals, but as Kenny Holtzman learned, the habits you form when you're young carry over as you get older. Form good habits now, and you should have little trouble keeping them up as you get older.

FULL WINDUP

When there is no one on base or only a man on third, you take what's called a *full windup*. "Full" means that your motion is one fluid movement from the time you begin until you complete your follow-through. There is really no such thing as "the right way" or "the wrong way" to wind up; whatever comes naturally and feels comfortable to you is the right way. You probably won't have any trouble with your windup if you don't force it or try to imitate anyone else. Don't worry if your windup doesn't look smooth. Many pitchers have what is called a "herky-jerky" motion, meaning they look awkward and unbalanced when they throw. Dick Hall acquired the nickname "Turkey Neck" because he constantly popped his head up and down

CONCENTRATION IS HALF THE BATTLE . . . when you begin the pitching windup. When I start my motion, all I think about is getting power and control behind the ball I'm about to throw.

THROWING THE BALL. You can see a step-by-step illustration of how I throw the ball, in the next five photos (*from left to right*). First, after assuming my stance on the rubber, taking one short step back with my left leg, raising my hands above my head, and swiveling my hips, I kick my left leg up into the air (*first photo*). Then (*second photo*) I kick my left leg out and start bringing the ball back. As I start to stretch my left leg to establish my stride (*third photo*), I start bringing the ball around. Then I stretch to my full stride and bring the ball up (*fourth photo*). I plant my left foot (*fifth photo*) and begin to bring the ball through from the back just before I release it.

as he pitched. Phil Regan was called "Peek-A-Boo" because he would peer at the batter over the top of his glove, and Don Larsen didn't even use a full windup when he pitched his perfect game in the 1956 World Series. As every major league pitcher will tell you, the object is to get people out, not to look good.

Let's go through the steps of a full windup, assuming you are right-handed. (Left-handed pitchers will do just the opposite.) Start with your right foot on the rubber, the ball in your glove (left hand), your hands at your sides, and shoulders squared and parallel to the pitching rubber. You may even be leaning forward just a bit. Take one short step backward with your left foot. At the same time shift your weight to the left foot and bring your arms up above your head, bending them slightly at the elbows, and touch your hands. Transfer the ball to your right hand and grip it. Then begin to move your body forward; shift your weight onto your right foot; and turn your entire body so that you are facing third base (this movement is called "swiveling your hips"). Kick your left leg up into the air as high as you can while still feeling comfortable and balanced, and begin pushing off the rubber with your right foot, while still keeping the toe firmly planted. As your body moves toward home plate, bring your arm around quickly and release the ball, following through by stepping forward with your right foot and extending your arm, wrist, and hand out in front of you. Your right foot should land in front of you, establishing a firm, balanced base.

How do you remember all this? After a few practices you won't have to; a pitching motion is a natural movement for the body. You shouldn't even be thinking about your pitching motion; you should be concentrating on the pitch you're about to throw.

I have a very short pitching motion. My shoulders form a parallel line with the rubber. I swing easily into my windup, swivel my hips toward third, give a short kick,

and follow through by bringing my right leg around. I like to compare my pitching motion to syrup running down a plate—smooth and easy.

But one word of warning: don't copy my full windup—it might not work for you. Do what feels comfortable and natural and once you've decided what feels comfortable, stick with it. You can give your pitch away by changing your pitching motion even slightly, as I found out. When I came up to the major leagues, I would bite my tongue every time I threw a curve ball. As soon as a hitter saw my tongue, bells would start ringing. Pitching coach Cal McLish picked up on this habit of mine while I was with Philadelphia. Needless to say I stopped doing it.

STRETCH MOTION

When there are runners on base, you should pitch from what is called the *stretch position.* The stretch motion is broken down into two parts: the first part, coming to the *set position,* and the second part, or the actual throwing movement. The object of pitching from the stretch is to keep runners close to the base they occupy. Since you can turn and throw to any base from the set position, no smart runner will wander too far from a base until you've committed yourself to throwing to the plate.

I begin the stretch motion by placing the right side of my right foot against the front of the pitching rubber. My body is facing third base, and my shoulders bisect the pitching rubber vertically. When I'm taking the signal from the catcher, I lean toward the plate. The ball is in my glove, and my glove is resting on my left leg. Then I bring my glove up to my belt, grip the ball with my pitching hand, stand up straight, and pause. This is known as the set position, and from there I can turn my head and see where the runner is. If he has taken too big a lead, I can throw over to hold him closer.

From the set position I swing into the throwing motion, which is much like the full windup except that I save time (to prevent the runner from getting a jump) by not bringing my hands over my head. Instead I just kick my left leg up, reach back, push off the rubber, and fire home. The *follow-through* is exactly the same as in a regular pitch. There are minor variations of the stretch, which will be explained, but pitching from a stretch position should be just as easy and natural as pitching from a full windup. If you let your body do the work, it will be automatic, just like walking around the block.

With a Man on First

I use the basic stretch motion when there's a man on first, but some other pitchers cheat a little. As they bring their hands to their belt in the set position, they take a short step with their left foot toward first base, so that the front of their body is parallel to the third base foul line. These pitchers feel that this maneuver makes it easier for them to turn and throw to first base. Left-handed throwers have a natural advantage with a man on first, but they have to be careful with a man on third and might cheat a bit in that situation.

With a Man on Second

I usually pause just a second or so longer in the set position with a man on second than I would with a man on first, because I want to keep the man on second as close to the base as possible, so that we might get a play at home plate if the batter gets a hit.

With a Man on Third

If the base runner on third is the only man on base, you can either pitch from a stretch or take a full windup. What I do usually depends on who the runner is. If it's someone like Lou Brock, who might try to steal home, I'll go to the stretch to hold him close. I also will stretch if I think the *suicide squeeze* or *safety bunt* might be on. If you keep the runner close to his base, you can often prevent him from scoring on an infield grounder.

DELIVERY

The angle at which you bring your arm over your shoulder is called the *angle of delivery,* or your *delivery.* There are three basic deliveries: *full overhand, three-quarter overhand,* and *sidearm.* A fourth style of delivery, called a *submarine,* pops up every once in a while.

There really is not much difference between the three basic deliveries in terms of what they make the ball do. I suggest you

A THREE-QUARTER OVERHAND . . . is my natural delivery. Although this is the most comfortable delivery for me, you should use the delivery that is easiest for you.

try them all, decide what feels most comfortable, and work on the one you like best. A pitcher's arm takes a great deal of punishment under the best circumstances, and if you start fooling around with different deliveries, you'll be putting an additional, unnecessary strain on it.

My natural delivery is a three-quarter overhand. Every few months I analyze my delivery and decide that I'd do better against left-handed hitters if I delivered a full overhand. Then I think about what happened to the great Dizzy Dean. Pitching in an All-Star game, Dizzy suffered a broken foot. To compensate for the pain he changed his delivery, strained his arm, and was never the same. Needless to say, I still throw a three-quarter overhand against all hitters.

Full Overhand

In this delivery, the arm is brought straight back over the shoulder and returns in a position almost vertical to the ground. Many pitching coaches feel that a full overhand delivery enables a pitcher to use all the power in his shoulders. Hitters usually like to face pitchers who throw a full overhand because the ball comes straight in rather than on an angle.

Three-quarter

I've always thrown a three-quarter overhand, and I think this delivery helps me to get the ball to sink a little easier. Also, a ball thrown from a three-quarter overhand comes at the hitter from an angle and makes it a little tougher to hit.

Sidearm

There aren't as many sidewinders, as the sidearm pitcher is called, around as there used to be. I've never really liked the side-arm delivery because I can't get my body behind the pitch, so I lose a little velocity. But a good sidearm pitcher will have batters *stepping in the bucket* all day long. Lefty Steve Hamilton was one of the great sidearm specialists of all time. He's about 6'7", and he'd lean way over to the right to throw his pitch. Hamilton was devastating against left-handed hitters because when he threw, it must have looked as if the ball was coming from behind the first base coach.

Submarine

The submarine is an unusual delivery, and the few pitchers I've seen using it have chosen it after suffering a sore arm. The major advantage of a submarine delivery is that batters see it so rarely that they have a tough time getting used to it. A good submarine pitcher will make his fast ball drop and his curve ball rise (the opposite of what they usually do) and give really good hitters a tough time. I have seen Ted Abernathy, one of the best submarine pitchers, make Willie Mays look sick at bat—and then get racked by the seventh, eighth, and ninth batters. I really don't recommend experimenting with a submarine delivery because it puts a great strain on your arm and takes much of the velocity off the ball.

FOLLOW-THROUGH

Ted Williams teaches that every hitter should try to hit every pitch directly up the middle. For a hitter that's good advice, but for a pitcher it means disaster because he is the only one standing in the ball's way. All season long a pitcher takes constant abuse —balls come whistling between his legs, over his shoulder, or next to his head. Occasionally, as in the case of Herb Score, who was almost blinded by a line drive, pitchers do get hit. Every pitcher on the mound can be hit by the ball, but to worry about it is foolish and time-consuming. If you follow through correctly after releasing the ball, you eliminate a lot of the danger and you prevent yourself from losing control.

Striding

The distance between the foot that is on the rubber (the right if you are right-handed) and the front foot after you have finished kicking (the left if you are right-handed) is called your stride. If you take too long or

THE STRIDE . . . is the distance between the foot that is on the rubber (the back foot in the photo) and the front foot after you have finished kicking. My stride is quite long because I am tall and can stretch a good distance while still feeling comfortable.

too short a stride you will have control problems because you will either be reaching (too long a stride) or holding back (too short a stride). In both cases you'll be off balance and unprepared to protect yourself. After you finish your delivery, your feet should form a solid, balanced base that puts you in a position to look directly at home plate. Your feet should be somewhat even so that you can get momentum to go forward if you have a fielding play in front of you. If you keep your eyes on the target and your head steady, you should not have any major problems with your stride. It may be a bit long or a bit short, but that is easily corrected.

Protecting Yourself

I've been hit by batted balls many times, but the worst was in 1969. Willie Crawford of the Dodgers hit a line drive back at me, and I wasn't ready for it. I managed to *tip* the ball with my glove, but it hit my pitching hand hard. By the time the trainer got to the mound, my thumb was swollen to twice its normal size, and I thought it was broken. I was lucky, though; it was just badly bruised, and I missed only one game. But now I remember a cardinal rule for pitchers: keep your hands *up* at all times!

There is little you can do to protect yourself besides being ready. However, you should be aware that some batters hit up the middle more often than others. If you're pitching to a batter with good power to the *opposite field* and you're throwing him outside, you know there is a good chance that the ball will come back at you.

If you're playing in a ball park with seats behind home plate, be careful. In Montreal, for example, there are silver seats behind home plate; after it rains, you can't see a thing. In Los Angeles people frequently wear white shirts; when they sit behind the plate, you easily can lose the ball off the bat. Then it seems as if everything that is fouled straight back is coming right at you. Don't take anything for granted in that kind of situation. The ball you think is foul may be the one that hits you. Protect yourself at all times.

The final thing you can do to help protect yourself is to play lots of *pepper games*. In a pepper game one hitter and at least one fielder stand two or three yards apart. The fielder throws, and the ball is hit right back at him. As pitcher, you should work on your pepper game and become really good because it helps you to get the quick reaction you need to play the ball coming off the bat—in the end your best protection will be your own reaction to the ball.

THE BEST WEAPON YOU HAVE . . . when you are on the mound is your ability to make the ball do the unexpected. The mark of a good pitcher is often determined by the variety of pitches he is able to throw. The larger your pitching repertoire, the more you are able to throw the "unexpected" ball.

chapter 3
DEVELOPING A REPERTOIRE AND CONTROL

Consider the poor pitcher, standing out there alone on the mound. The fans are screaming for action; they want to see the batter hit the ball. The other team has only one goal in mind: your destruction. So it's you alone. As I said before, you have only one weapon—the baseball. Until you decide you're ready to wind up and throw, nothing will happen. But once you release the ball, it's anybody's game. The more unexpected things you can make that baseball do between your release of it and its arrival at home plate—the more times you can make it hop, drop, skip, skim, spin, rise, and drop—the better off you'll be. Even a fast ball has to "move" if you're going to get anybody out with it. And the way you make a fast ball rise, a curve ball drop, a change-up slow down, or a slider slide depends on the way you grip the ball and the way you hold it in your hand as you release

it. The air hitting the laces as the ball speeds toward home plate does the rest.

It is extremely important that you learn the basic grips early in your career, even if you might not want to use them all. Knowing all the proper ways to grip the ball will keep you from getting into bad habits and knocked out of ball games. The basic pitching repertoire of a young pitcher varies. It should include a fast ball, a *change-up,* and perhaps a slider. I don't think you should try to throw a hard curve ball until you have fully developed. I've heard of more than one instance in which a young pitcher ruined his arm by trying to throw breaking pitches too often or incorrectly at too early an age. Specialty pitches such as the *knuckle ball* and the *sinker* are a little different. They can be thrown with almost no strain on the arm, so if you can get them to work for you, use them.

FAST BALL

When Jim Bouton, author of *Ball Four*, was with the Yankees, he would throw his fast ball so hard that he would lose his cap. Of course, once he lost his fast ball he didn't have to worry about losing his cap anymore—his career was just about over.

The fast ball is to a pitcher what the home run is to a hitter. It's the "big" one, the money pitch, the pitch that wins ball games. A lot of pitchers have lasted a long time in the majors without a great fast ball, but when you name the greatest pitchers in recent baseball history—Sandy Koufax, Juan Marichal, Bob Gibson, Tom Seaver, Bob Feller, and Vida Blue—you're talking about fast ball pitchers. You don't have to be a physical giant to throw a good fast ball; actually it's one of the easiest pitches to throw correctly. All it takes is the proper grip, release, and follow-through.

I consider myself a fast ball pitcher, and I depend on it when I'm in a jam. There isn't a single hitter in the major leagues that I'd be afraid to challenge with it— because I know it will move. If all a fast ball did was to come in right over the plate, even at over 90 miles per hour, it would not be hard to hit. Even Ferguson Jenkins'

FOR RIGHT-HANDED HITTERS . . . I grip my fast ball *across* the seams, because I want the ball to stay inside.

FOR LEFT-HANDED HITTERS . . . I grip my fast ball *along* the seams, because I want the ball to move a little faster than it does when I throw to a right-handed hitter.

fast ball would be easy to hit if it didn't move. So you have to make it hop, sink, or sail.

I throw two different kinds of fast balls, one to right-handed hitters and another to left-handed ones. When a right-handed hitter is at bat, I want the ball to stay inside. I don't want it out over the middle of the plate where he can get good wood on the ball. I want to jam him, or lock his hands in. So I grip the ball directly across the seams and throw it. The action of the air currents on the laces causes the ball to hop before it reaches the batter.

When a left-handed hitter is at the plate, I want the ball to move a little more than I do for a right-handed hitter. I want it to be right on his hands before it either hops or drops. So I grip the ball along the seams. In both cases I tuck my thumb under the ball.

When I'm winding up to throw the fast ball to either a right- or left-handed hitter, I hold the ball in my hand about the same way, firmly but comfortably. I don't squeeze it because if I hold it too tightly, I'll end up throwing it right into the dirt. The release for a fast ball is very simple. I let the ball slide out of my hand naturally and follow through with my wrist. To help me develop the necessary overhand action for delivering a fast ball and to help me build up my back muscles, Gene Dziadura, the man who signed me to a contract with Philadelphia, bought me a brand new axe and had me chop wood. The action I need in bringing the axe over my shoulder is the same action I use to deliver my fast ball.

THE CURVE BALL . . . is gripped with the middle finger running along the seam of the ball and the index finger resting on the cover.

CURVE BALL

There is a famous baseball story about a rookie who hit .800 the first three weeks of spring training. Then he sent a letter home. "Dear Mom," he wrote, "I'll be home next week. They're starting to throw curve balls." The action of a curve ball is just what it sounds like: when thrown by a right-handed pitcher it curves away from a right-handed batter and into a lefty. A left-handed pitcher's curve ball does just the opposite. A good curve ball, like the one Camilo Pasquel threw when he was in the majors, does more than curve; it actually drops very sharply. When Pasquel threw a curve, it dropped so sharply that it looked as if someone had rolled a baseball off the edge of a table. Candy Cummings, who invented the curve ball just before the turn of the century, is the patron saint of pitchers, in a manner of speaking. There are still some scientists who say that the curve ball doesn't actually curve—it's just an optical illusion. Tell that to Billy Williams and see what he says.

The curve is gripped with the middle finger running along the seam, or laces, of the ball and index finger resting on the cover. The middle finger on the seam exerts more pressure on the ball than does the index finger.

You throw a curve in much the same way that you would pull down a window shade. With your hand on top of the ball, you reach out with your arm extended, and pull down the window shade, snapping the wrist down quickly. The pressure of the middle finger on the lace causes the ball to spin in such a way that it curves.

The curve ball results from a simple pulling action. You need strong wrists to throw it. To help me strengthen my wrists Dziadura brought me a five-pound sledgehammer, and for months he had me hammering on concrete blocks or hammering nails into wood. The curve ball is executed with almost exactly the same wrist motion as that used for hammering.

A curve ball is a great pitch to throw to a good fast ball hitter because it comes up on him much like a fast ball and then starts to break. A good curve is an important pitch, but until you have developed your wrist and forearm, it's also a dangerous pitch because it puts a strain on your arm. I suggest practicing with a hammer before you try to throw a curve ball.

CHANGE-UP

In one of his baseball diaries Jim Brosnan wrote about a game against the Cubs. He said that the last time he had faced the Cubs, Ernie Banks had hit a tremendous home run off a change-up. The next time, Brosnan thought, he would experiment by throwing Banks a change-up on the first pitch. He figured that there was no way Ernie could be expecting it. Unfortunately, Jim was wrong. Ernie's eyes lit up when he saw the change-up coming, and he put it over the wall.

This story is a perfect example of the danger of throwing a change-of-pace ball at the wrong moment. The object is to use a change-up to throw a batter's timing off. If the batter is waiting for it, however, you're in trouble. The change-up is a good pitch to throw to great fast ball hitters, players that really can wallop the ball. We threw everything except the kitchen sink at Johnny Bench until we discovered he had trouble with off-speed pitches such as the change-up. We used it, and his average immediately took a nose dive.

Changing up simply means taking some of the velocity off the ball. Change-ups come in medium, slow, and even slower speeds, anything that will upset a hitter's timing. The change-up is thrown with the same motion as a fast ball, and the pressure on the ball is precisely the same. The grip is what makes the difference between the change-up and the fast ball. I grip my change-up away from the seams. I spread my fingers very wide; I suppose you might call my version a *fork ball* (Diagram 4) change-up. I hold the ball so that even though I'm throwing it as I would throw a fast ball, I don't get all my power behind it. Other pitchers choke the ball between their thumb and forefinger or grip it with the entire palm wrapped around the ball. The best thing to do is find a way that works for you.

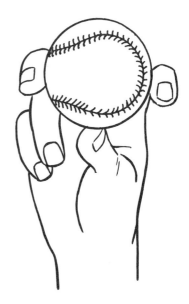

DIAGRAM 4. Fork ball.

MY VERSION OF THE CHANGE-UP . . . is really a fork ball change-up. I grip the ball away from the seams and spread my fingers very wide so that I don't get all my power behind the ball.

A word of warning: a change-up is only effective as part of a pitching pattern. You have to set a batter up for it by throwing some hard stuff first. On the other hand, it's an excellent *waste pitch*. Letting a batter look at a change-up off the plate can ruin his timing and set him up for a fast ball.

SLIDER

First they put the rabbit in the baseball and made it livelier; then they lowered the mound. But whatever they do, they can't take away the slider. Pitchers call the slider "the great equalizer." It comes up on the plate looking exactly like a fast ball, and then, just as the batter begins to swing, it slides across the plate; it might even drop a little.

Like a change-up, a slider is part of a pitching pattern; it is best thrown when a hitter is waiting to feast upon a fast ball. Actually, the slider is a little tougher pitch to throw than the fast ball or change-up; Its success depends totally on your wrist action. A slider is gripped like a fast ball and thrown off the same motion, but it varies from the fast ball in that during the follow-through your fingers slide off the seams. When you finish your follow-through, your thumb should be pointing upward.

The slider is best thrown when the count is 2-1 or 2-2. Because the slider does have a tendency to drop, you throw it when you want the batter to hit the ball on the ground. A slider is also a good strike-out pitch, and most of all it is great for the pitcher's ego—he knows that he has completely fooled the batter.

SPECIALTY PITCHES

The fast ball, curve ball, change-up, and slider are considered the "big four" of any pitcher's repertoire. Before you begin to experiment with secondary pitches, you should be able to throw all of the four or any combination of them (the change-up curve is a great pitch) to a given spot on the plate. When you can consistently hit the black edges of the plate with all of the big four pitches, you're ready to move on to the secondary pitches. The first thing to remember about these specialty pitches is that not everyone can throw them. Mastery of any one of them might be enough to earn you a spot on a major league roster—for example, Hoyt Wilhelm with his butterfly knuckler. But even before you start throwing any of the following specialty pitches, try getting the ball to move easily in different directions. Remember, you can make the ball move in, out, up, or down by simply putting pressure on the ball in different spots.

KNUCKLE BALL

Because it is so difficult to control, the knuckle ball (Diagram 5) is the most difficult specialty pitch to throw, but it can be the best. The knuckle ball is the most unpredictable of all pitches; it might rise, drop, or break in or out. The batter has absolutely no idea of what the knuckle ball will do when it reaches the plate. Unfortunately, neither do the pitcher and catcher. The knuckle ball leads to a lot of passed balls, and most catchers use a special oversized mitt when a knuckle baller is pitching. It's a dangerous pitch to throw with men on bases unless, like Hoyt Wilhelm, you can put it in the strike zone consistently. If you can control the knuckle ball, it's worth throwing because it puts almost no strain on your arm. And even if the batter's waiting for the knuckle ball, chances are he won't be able to hit it. I've seen three totally different types of knuckle balls: Phil Niekro, a starting pitcher, throws a hard

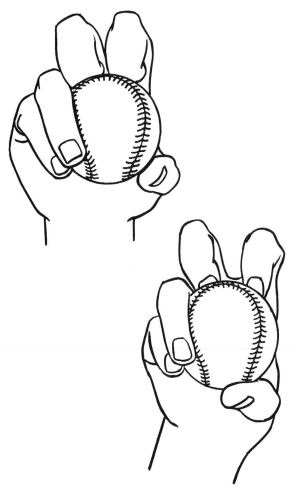

DIAGRAM 5. Two versions of the knuckle ball.

knuckler; Hoyt Wilhelm, whom the Giants gave up on in the late 1950s because he was too old and who almost pitched the Dodgers to the pennant in 1971, throws a floater, a butterfly ball; and young Burt Hooten throws an amazing knuckle-curve ball. The knuckler is thrown off of any pitching motion, and the trick is to prevent the ball from spinning even the slightest bit. The knuckle ball is totally at the mercy of the air currents; it doesn't need any spin. If it is thrown correctly, you can watch it dance to home plate.

There are many different ways of throwing the knuckle ball, and whatever works for you is the best. Wilhelm digs his fingernails into the ball and pushes it out of his hand. Others fold their fingers over, press their knuckles against the top of the ball, and fling it out of their hands. Still others grip it by their fingertips and float it out toward home plate. There is no "correct" way of throwing a knuckler. You'll know you've discovered your best method when the ball does not spin at all.

SINKER

The sinker can give an old pitcher a new life, or give a new pitcher no life at all. Because throwing the sinker involves a little backward twist of your wrist and consequently puts a real strain on your arm, it may not be worth learning how to throw it until you have had considerable pitching experience. But if you're not getting anyone out with the pitches you're throwing, or if you throw a natural sinker, as Bob Lemon used to, it's a valuable pitch to know. The sinker is aptly named; it comes right up to the batter and dips quickly, usually causing him to bang the ball into the ground. Because the batter can't get a decent hit off of it, the sinker is a big favorite of relief pitchers who come out of the bullpen needing a double play to get out of a jam. When the ball sinks, you're a hero; when it doesn't sink, the sinker is a medium-speed fast ball, and you're going to get burned.

The sinker is thrown off a straight overhand motion. The ball is gripped across the laces, like a fast ball, but the thumb is tucked directly under the ball. Your wrist should be slightly turned toward third base (first base if you're throwing left-handed) as you throw. The idea is to grip the ball tightly with your fingers and, as you release the ball, to pull back on the laces. This maneuver creates a backspin, causing the ball to drop sharply. I don't throw the sinker simply because I have a great deal

THE SINKER . . . is gripped across the laces, like a fast ball, but the thumb is tucked directly under the ball. In gripping the ball your wrist should be slightly turned toward third base if you're throwing right-handed, first base if you're throwing left-handed.

of success with the basic pitches, and I don't want to take a chance on hurting my business interest.

SCREWBALL

Luis Arroyo won fame, fortune, and a pennant for the Yankees as a *screwball* specialist. He could come out of the bullpen and throw his scroogie with great success, but he paid the price off the field. Because of the terrific pressure that throwing the screwball placed on his elbow, Arroyo's arm was permanently twisted out of shape.

The screwball is a reverse curve. Thrown by a right-handed pitcher it breaks down and in on a right-handed batter and away from a left-handed one. But unless everything else has failed, I don't recommend trying to throw this pitch. It is thrown with the same windup and arm action as all the

rest of your pitches. It is gripped exactly the reverse of the way in which you grip your curve ball—your forefinger is on the inside lace, or seam, and your middle finger rests on the cover of the ball. As you release the screwball, turn your wrist, elbow, and forearm toward first base so that you end up with your palm facing third base. This twist of your hand and arm gives the ball the overspin on one side that causes the ball to break in the opposite direction from a regular curve.

NOVELTY PITCHES

Every once in a while a pitcher will invent a new pitch or revive one that hasn't been used in many years. We call these pitches *novelty pitches,* and few big leaguers will even experiment with them unless all else has failed. Long Steve Hamilton brought new life to Rip Sewell's old blooper pitch recently, but he threw it more for fun than for pitching profit. On the other hand, Elroy Face carved a career for himself by gripping the ball between his forefinger and middle finger, flipping it easily toward home plate, and consistently dazzling hitters with his fork ball. The best known novelty pitches are the *palm ball,* the *slip pitch,* and the *blooper,* but there are many more. Most of these pitches were discovered during experiments in practice sessions.

If you want to try to invent a novelty pitch, grip the ball comfortably, apply different amounts of pressure to different parts of the ball with various parts of your hand, throw the ball, and see what happens. In conducting these experiments be careful not to strain your arm. You easily can prevent strain by avoiding unnatural arm movements. I don't suggest throwing any sort of novelty pitch in a game unless you've had tremendous success in practice sessions and can consistently get the ball over the plate.

THE BASICS OF CONTROL

The ability to throw many different types of pitches is only half the battle in becoming a good pitcher. The other half is being able to put the ball where you want it to go — what we call *control.* I cannot overemphasize the importance of pitching control. Having the quickest pitching gun in the majors will do you no good at all unless you can pitch to the same spot consistently. Knowing a batter's weakness is worthless unless your control is good enough to take advantage of those weaknesses. When I was 16 years old, Gene Dziadura set up a pair of badminton standards and measured off a 15-inch strike zone with two pieces of rope. Day after day, from the time I was

16 until I was 21, during the winter months in Chatham, I practiced throwing into those ropes. We would move them up and down and in and out to represent both left- and right-handed hitters of all sizes. After four years of cringing every time the ball hit the standards I finally developed reasonably good control. Today I can aim at the black edges of the plate and hit them with every different pitch I throw. The umpires know this, and they respect me enough that now they often give me credit for a pitch that is an inch or so off the plate. Good control does wonders for your confidence and your earned run average.

Don't worry if you can't always throw the ball where you want to. Even experienced pitchers can have streaks of wildness. I remember a game against the Phillies in 1968 in which I gave up a home run and started talking to myself. What happened is that I stopped thinking; I stopped concentrating on my job. Boom! I hit the next batter. I walked the next three hitters in a row, forced in a run, and lost the ball game. But I learned another important lesson from that experience: control problems are correctable. Now when I start getting wild, I usually will walk off the mound and ask Don Kessinger or Glen Beckert if they can detect what I'm doing wrong. Am I throwing too quickly? Taking too long a stride? Releasing the ball too early? Gripping the ball too tight? Taking my eyes off the catcher? Not following through?

Control problems are identifiable and correctable as long as you know what you are supposed to be doing. There are two basics of good control. First, develop one motion and don't ever vary it, so that whatever you're doing differently that is causing control problems can be isolated and corrected. Second, never take your eyes off the catcher's glove. When I swing my arms over my head, my eyes are in exactly the same place as they were when I started my windup, and my eyes will be in that same place when I follow through. There are some very rare individuals, such as Vernon Law or Mudcat Grant, who pitch without watching the catcher, but these pitchers have natural control. You probably are not that lucky.

Control problems are indicated not only when you can't get the ball over the plate (and believe me that old cliché is true — *walks* do come back to haunt you) but also when you put the ball over the wrong part of the plate. It does no good to know that Ron Santo doesn't particularly like inside pitches if you can't keep the ball inside. Earl Williams reminded me of this on the "Game of the Week" one Saturday afternoon. I threw a slider to him and didn't get it down where I wanted it; he hit it out of the park and beat me 3-2.

Some control problems are mental. When you lose confidence in your ability, you're in real trouble. When I walk out to the mound, I know that I'm the best; if I did not think so, I wouldn't be pitching. But other control problems are mechanical, and these usually are caused by a simple, correctable mistake. Try to analyze what you are doing wrong; then take the proper steps to correct your control problems.

CORRECTING CONTROL PROBLEMS

Too high—A too-high pitch usually is caused by one of two problems: either you're taking too long a stride during your follow-through or you're releasing the ball too early (too high). Try shortening your stride first, and if that doesn't work, speed up your pitching motion — make your arm come around a little quicker. Also make sure that you're not striding into a hole.

Too low—A too-low pitch results from just the opposite reasons for a too-high pitch: your stride is too short, or you're coming around too quickly. Take a little more time on the mound—don't try to rush things. Take your natural stride at an easy pace.

Inside or outside—Throwing inside or outside usually means you're taking your eyes off your target. You may be looking at the hitter and throwing to him rather than to your catcher. You may also be gripping the ball a little too loosely and therefore not getting the proper finger action. Keep your eyes where they should be and think about what you're doing.

Wild pitch—A wild pitch is caused by any number of factors: taking your eyes off your target, panicking during your windup and trying to speed up, gripping the ball incorrectly, or even trying to "over throw" the ball by putting too much on the pitch and bouncing it in the dirt. If you slow down and relax, you won't throw too many wild pitches.

CHECKLIST OF PITCHING FAULTS

If you're having trouble getting the ball in the same area consistently, you're probably making one or two basic mistakes. If you think about what you're doing, you'll be able to overcome your problems. Control can be learned. If you are having control problems, mentally go through this checklist; it will serve as a guide to help you find out what's wrong.

1. Wrong position on the rubber: You may be pitching from either side of the rubber or off the top. Pitching from the side means you're crossfiring and may be dropping your arm. If you're standing on the top of the rubber, you don't have a good base from which to push off. If you're standing properly on the rubber, only the outside edge of your right spike will be touching the front of the rubber.

IF I'M HAVING CONTROL PROBLEMS . . . I mentally go through the list of things that possibly could be throwing me off. However, don't spend too much time going through the checklist of pitching faults when you are on the mound; save the real work for practice sessions.

2. Gripping the ball improperly: As we've discussed, if you're holding the ball either too loosely or too firmly, you won't be able to put the ball where you choose. The best grip is a comfortable one, with slight pressure where you want it

3. Speed of your windup: You may be rushing the ball to the plate, or perhaps you are being lazy. This will cause you to be too high or too low. Just think about what you're doing and speed up or slow down—whatever is necessary.

4. Overstriding or understriding: Check to make sure you're not stepping into a hole, and examine the speed of your windup.

5. Lack of follow-through: You may not be bending your back when you throw, and this can cause all sorts of problems. Make sure that your arm actually reaches for the ground after you have released the ball.

6. Not watching the target: You can't hit what you don't see. Keep your eyes on the catcher's glove.

7. Throwing across your body: The momentum of your pitch may be pulling you across to one side of the mound. When you finish your pitch, your front foot should be aimed at your target. If it is not, you're probably throwing across your body and probably dropping your arm. Just concentrate on stepping toward the target.

8. Overthrowing: You may be trying too hard. Relax and concentrate. You don't have to throw hard to win — just throw accurately.

9. Physical condition: Pitching takes a lot out of you. Toward the end of a game you may become tired. Try taking more time between pitches. If that doesn't work, let your manager know that you are exhausted. And keep in shape.

10. Lack of self-control: Don't get mad at yourself and lose your self-control; in the long run it will cost you more than it is worth. Scouts look very carefully to see if a young player can keep his poise when things are rough.

11. Lack of confidence: Before I throw the first pitch, I stand out on the mound and say to myself, "Fergie, this team simply cannot beat you." Confidence is tremendously important. If you don't have it, you'll be afraid to challenge hitters, and you'll end up in the showers.

PITCHING STRATEGY . . . sounds simple enough, but what is really involved is far more compli-cated. You must know the hitting patterns of each and every batter who comes up in front of you; you must be able to confuse the hitter and throw him the ball he doesn't expect; and you must be able to work with your catcher.

chapter 4
STRATEGY

In terms of getting the ball over the plate with some speed on it, the best pitcher I've ever seen is a nuts and bolts machine named "Iron Mike." Mike literally has a rubber arm and can throw all day — hard, soft, inside, outside, fast balls, curves — whatever you want. We use Mike for batting practice. But there is much more to pitching than just getting the ball over the plate with something on it. If there weren't, we would make Mike our pitcher. Mike may be able to get a ball across the plate every time, but you have something he lacks: a brain. A winning pitcher has learned to think and concentrate while on the mound. He has a constant flow of data clicking through his mind: the strengths and weaknesses of the hitter, what he did last time up, how many men are on base, the habits of the umpire, etc.

Reaction to the data that are moving through your brain when you are on the mound is called strategy. Good baseball strategy wins games and keeps earned run averages down. I know some pitchers who take a magic marker and write the word THINK on the back of their glove. I don't think that it is necessary to write it though; just remember to do it.

STRIKE ZONE

You have to know what the *strike zone* is before you can use it to your advantage. The rule book describes it as "that space over home plate which is between the batter's armpits and the top of his knees when he assumes his natural stance." In other words, it's not a very big area. If you can't recognize instantly every batter's strike zone when he is up at bat, you've defeated your entire purpose for being on the mound. You can be sure that every hitter knows his strike zone. Many batters go into unnatural crouches to reduce their strike zone and make good pitches harder to throw. If you don't use the limits of the strike zone to your advantage, it won't be long before your manager takes you out of the game.

The person who really took advantage of the size of a hitter's strike zone was Bill Veeck. When Veeck was the general manager of the St. Louis Browns, he sent a midget up to bat. The midget immediately crouched over and established the smallest strike zone in history — about three inches. Needless to say, the hitter walked on four pitches.

Keeper of the Strike Zone

At the turn of the century there was a sign hanging in the Chicago ball park that read, "Please do not shoot the umpire. He is doing the best job he can." The *umpire* is the keeper of the strike zone, he decides what the strike zone is. Sometimes you and the umpire will have varying opinions on this matter, but until they change the rules and let pitchers call their own pitches, there's nothing you can do but go along with him.

Every umpire is different, and it's tough to know how each one is going to call individual strike zones. I know the low and high ball umpires. Doug Harvey and Billy Williams in the National League, for example, are excellent low ball umpires. (American League umpires stand straight behind the catcher; National League umpires crouch down over one shoulder. Consequently, there is a lower strike zone in the National League.) Even though I see the same umpires every so often, there are very few times when I can say to myself, "I can throw a pitch right there because I know this umpire is going to give it to me."

A HITTER'S STRIKE ZONE . . . as described by the rule book is "that space over home plate which is between the batter's armpits and the top of his knees when he assumes his natural stance" (the area indicated by the white-lined box in the photograph).

So what I try to do is get a good idea of the umpire's strike zone in the first two innings and use this knowledge when I throw my pitches. For example, it is important to know as early as possible in a game that an umpire won't give you the high inside strike so that you will not throw high inside when you need a strike.

Moving the Pitch Around

Once you know where the strike zone is, you can take advantage of it. Every hitter has certain strengths, and most have blind spots, or areas in the strike zone that they don't cover well. To find a hitter's blind spot move the ball around, in and out, up and down, until you discover it. However, when you move the ball around, remember that most hitters like to go after the ball when it is up in the strike zone, between the thighs and the stomach, so try to stay away from that area.

PSYCHING YOURSELF UP

Usually you don't have to worry about getting yourself mentally ready for a game. There is a certain excitement, an air of expectation that automatically starts your adrenalin flowing. When I am scheduled to pitch, I can't wait to get out to the mound. But I don't consider any of this natural excitement "psyching myself up." I'm fully aware that the hitters are there to do their job, but I have enough confidence in my ability to believe that I can do my job better than they can do theirs. That attitude is what I mean by psyching yourself up. The key word is confidence. Believe in yourself because if you don't, no one else will.

On a day that I'm pitching I arrive at the ball park about an hour later than I usually do on practice days (because I won't be running to warm up), and I dress slowly. I lie down and mentally go over the oppo-

sition's batting order, from top to bottom, noting the first right- and left-handed pinch hitters. Then I'm ready.

PSYCHING OUT A BATTER

I have often heard baseball described as a game of the mind, and hitting has been defined as a science; I think both definitions are accurate. Baseball is as much a mental game as a physical game. Thought power has as much to do with winning as does muscle power. Every pitcher has a game plan, and every batter has one, too. The pitcher and hitter constantly are trying to outguess each other; needless to say, the one who wins this battle of wits has a distinct advantage.

It takes a smart pitcher to disrupt a hitter's train of thought. Batters tend to think in basic patterns. What did he throw me last time to get me out? What did I hit well? What pitch is working best for him today? What is he going to try to make me do? If the hitter can analyze the data and come up with the one right answer, knowing the pitch you're going to throw before you throw it, he has won the strategy battle.

To counter the hitter's data you must feed him false information. Let him think that you have lost your confidence, that your control is gone, that you are tired, or that you don't want to pitch to him. Confuse him as much as possible, and you'll be way ahead of him.

After watching Ryne Duren wipe his thick glasses and throw his first warmup pitch over the catcher's head to the *backstop,* few hitters could concentrate on anything more than staying alive. Bill Faul had his own device for outsmarting hitters. He thought that by wearing the numeral 13 and showing it to the batter after every pitch, it would make him think twice. It certainly worked on me—I began to think Bill Faul was crazy.

I don't know of a single hitter in the National League who doesn't believe that he can hit everything I can throw him, so I use any device I can think of to break a batter's confidence and thought patterns.

Shaking Off a Signal

Although every once in a while your catcher will signal for a pitch that you really don't want to throw, it's a good idea to shake off a catcher's sign just for the sake of appearances a few times every game. Usually you arrange beforehand to shake off a few catcher's signals;otherwise you'll be shaking off all of his signs until he comes back to his original one. Either way—with a pre-planned or unplanned shake-off — you're guaranteed to break the batter's concentration. I like to shake off a sign when a great hitter like Aaron or Clemente is at bat because they step out of the batter's box. One season Aaron came into Chicago on the tail of a 21-game hitting streak. The catcher and I made him step out of the box three times in a single turn at bat.

Often the catcher will remind you to shake off a sign by shaking his head or moving his glove. He shakes his head, and you respond by shaking your head. He moves his glove; you move your glove. By this time the batter will probably be shaking his head, and more often than not he will step out of the box.

Double Pumping

Double pumping occurs during your full windup. You swing your arms over your head to their peak, bring them back down, and then do it a second time. I don't double pump too often because it throws my timing off. But the point is that double pumping also throws the batter's timing off slightly and may break his concentration.

Stepping Off the Rubber

When a pitcher steps off the rubber, most batters think they've won the battle of wits because it looks as if the pitcher doesn't want to pitch, that he has lost confidence, or that conditions aren't right. Actually, stepping off the rubber is a very good way to make the batter wait—and think. And when he thinks, he begins to rethink his own conclusions about the pitch you are going to deliver. Chris Short spends a great deal of time making batters wait by playing with pebbles on the mound. So if you step off the rubber intentionally and make the batter wait, perhaps he won't be able to distinguish the intentional step-offs from the necessary ones.

Another way to create an impression of loss of confidence is to ask for a new ball. Asking for a new ball not only indicates to the batter that you are not ready, but it also takes time and makes the batter think he possibly has lost the edge he might have had with the other ball.

Speak to your catcher before the game about what he can do to disrupt a batter's thoughts. He can talk to the hitter, slow you down, walk out in front of the plate, change baseballs, and even argue with you.

KEEPING A BOOK ON HITTERS

It would be impossible to remember what every hitter in the league has done when you've pitched against him, but it is vitally important that you have this information.

To get information on hitters, all pitchers keep what is called a *pitching chart*. Diagram 6 is a chart that was kept when I pitched a game against the St. Louis Cardinals. (It is important to know in reading the pitching chart that each player on the field is assigned a position number: pitcher —1, catcher—2, first baseman—3, second baseman—4, third baseman—5, short stop —6, left fielder—7, center fielder—8, and

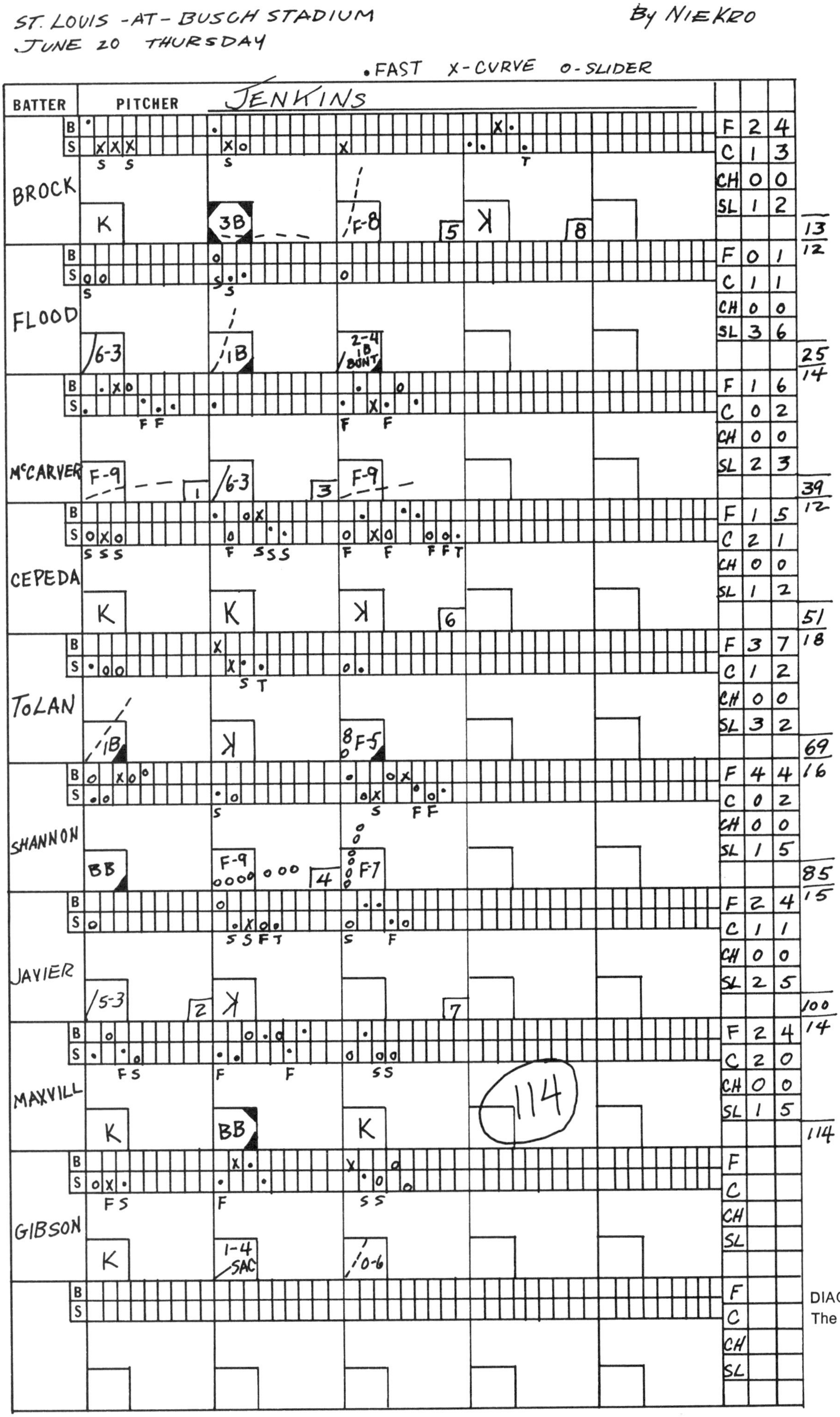

ST. LOUIS -AT- BUSCH STADIUM   By NIEKRO
JUNE 20 THURSDAY

• FAST   X - CURVE   O - SLIDER

BATTER	PITCHER	JENKINS						

BROCK — K — 3B — F-8 — 5 — K — 8
F 2 4 / C 1 3 / CH 0 0 / SL 1 2 — 13/12

FLOOD — 6-3 — 1B — 2-4 1B BUNT
F 0 1 / C 1 1 / CH 0 0 / SL 3 6 — 25/14

McCARVER — F-9 — 1 — 6-3 — 3 — F-9
F 1 6 / C 0 2 / CH 0 0 / SL 2 3 — 39/12

CEPEDA — K — K — K — 6
F 1 5 / C 2 1 / CH 0 0 / SL 1 2 — 51/18

TOLAN — 1B — K — 8 F-5
F 3 7 / C 1 2 / CH 0 0 / SL 3 2 — 69/16

SHANNON — BB — F-9 — 4 F-7
F 4 4 / C 0 2 / CH 0 0 / SL 1 5 — 85/15

JAVIER — 5-3 — 2 K — 7
F 2 4 / C 1 1 / CH 0 0 / SL 2 5 — 100/14

MAXVILL — K — BB — K — (114)
F 2 4 / C 2 0 / CH 0 0 / SL 1 5 — 114

GIBSON — K — 1-4 SAC — 0-6
F / C / CH / SL

B S / F C CH SL

DIAGRAM 6.
The pitching chart.

right fielder—9.) Phil Niekro, the pitcher who was scheduled to start against the Cards on the following day, kept the chart for me. Once you understand the symbols it's easy to read a pitching chart. Let's start right at the beginning. At the top of the chart you can see where Lou Brock, the leadoff hitter, took my first pitch—a high fast ball (·). The dot means fast ball, and the position of the dot in the box shows where it was thrown. After the first fast ball I threw Brock three straight low curves. He swung at and missed the first one (s); he took the second one as a called strike, and he struck out swinging on the third. The K in the large box indicates that Brock struck out swinging. If the K had been backward (Я), it would have indicated that the umpire called him out, as happened in the eighth inning (look at the fourth box in Brock's row). In the third inning I again opened with a fast ball against Brock, but this time it was low for ball one. Then Brock missed a curve and hit a slider (o) into right field for a triple. The broken line indicates the direction of the ball. If it had been a line of circles (ooooo), it would have indicated a fly ball. The filled-in corners of the bottom square indicate that Brock came home to score. The third time up I threw Brock a curve on the first pitch because I didn't want him to think that I'd throw him a fast ball on the first pitch every time he was up. He lined out to left field. The final time that Brock was up he took (T) a fast ball inside for strike three.

The list of numbers on the right-hand side of the page indicates how many pitches I threw (a total of 114), and what kind they were. I don't really remember this game too well, but by looking at this chart I can see that the Cardinals scored one run and didn't bat in the home half of the ninth, so they beat me 1-0. That's what happens when you're pitching against Bob Gibson.

Before every game the starting pitcher goes over his pitching charts to see who has been hitting well and what pitch he has been hitting.

The chart shown in Diagram 7 is used to indicate the areas of the field that a batter hits to. A hitter will be charted for an entire series on one diagram, with the symbols defined in the legend in the lower right-hand corner of the chart. If he consistently hits to one area of the field, the manager can position fielders in that area. Using both the pitcher's and hitter's charts, you can see that Tim McCarver (listed third on the pitcher's chart) lined out to right field on a fast ball in the first inning, grounded to short on an inside fast ball in the third, and flew out to right on a fast ball in the sixth. In the other two games of the series against the Cardinals, McCarver flew out to right once more, singled to right, had a ground ball single up the middle, and had a line drive out to second. Since the hitter's chart represents only seven at bats in a three-game series, McCarver presumably walked and struck out a few times. These charts give our team a great deal of knowledge that will be extremely useful the next time we face the Cardinals.

The third type of chart that pitchers keep is a mental one. Baseball players spend a tremendous amount of time off the field talking about baseball. They often get together to discuss which player is hitting which pitches and what might work against him. For example, Johnny Bench was hitting a home run against us almost every other game for a while. We thought that we had tried everything until someone suggested challenging him with off-speed pitches. The next time we faced him a relief pitcher threw him a change-up, and he almost ran up the line trying to hit the ball. We knew we had found his weakness. After that Johnny Bench saw nothing but soft stuff from Cub pitchers, and he began popping up all the time. Until Bench solves this problem, we have a good "book" on him.

The mental book you keep on hitters won't be as detailed as the charts we keep, but if you try keeping a record on the hitters over one season, you'll see how much it helps.

INTENTIONALLY PASSING

Although your job as a pitcher can be defined best as keeping the offensive team off the bases, sometimes it is to your advantage to put a man on base intentionally by throwing him four very wide pitches. If there are fewer than two out and there are men in scoring positions, for example, you might walk the batter to set up the possibility of a *double play* or a *force-out*, especially if

the batter is a good hitter. Never be afraid to put a man on base if you don't feel confident that you can get him out.

Another quite common strategy maneuver is the *semiintentional pass*. You pass a hitter semiintentionally by pitching near the plate—just close enough to interest him —but far enough away to prevent him from getting good wood on the ball. A semiintentional pass also is known as "pitching around a hitter," which a smart picher will do whenever the situation calls for it. You don't have to challenge every hitter that comes up, and you prove only one thing by pitching to a good hitter when you don't have to—that you haven't learned how to think on the mound.

The one thing to be careful of when intentionally or semiintentionally walking a hitter is getting the ball too close to the

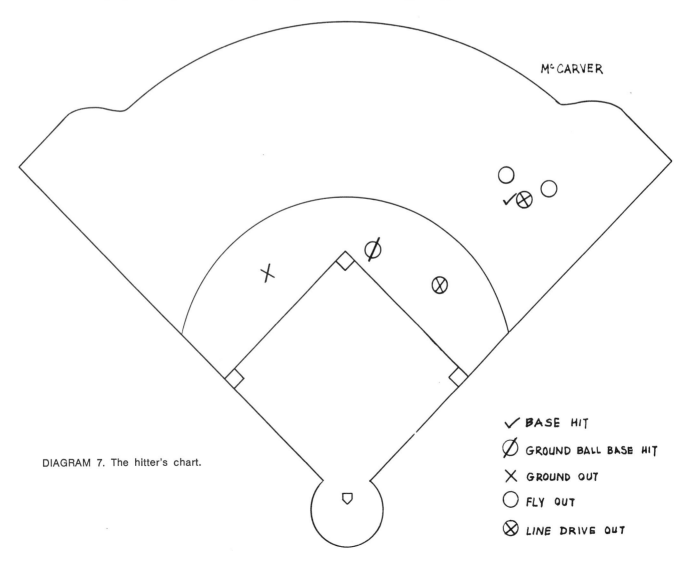

DIAGRAM 7. The hitter's chart.

✓ BASE HIT

⊘ GROUND BALL BASE HIT

✗ GROUND OUT

◯ FLY OUT

⊗ LINE DRIVE OUT

plate. I remember seeing Milt Pappas throw a 2-0 pitch to Doug Rader that was less than a foot outside. Rader reached out and poked it over second for two runs and the ball game.

WASTING A PITCH

Just as you don't have to get every batter out, you don't have to get every pitch over the plate. Sometimes, in fact, it is to your advantage to waste a pitch. The expression "wasting a pitch" means intentionally throwing the pitch well inside or far enough outside to discourage the batter from swinging. A waste pitch can be used to break a batter's train of thought and ruin his timing. I like to waste a pitch, sometimes even two, when I'm ahead 0-2, or 1-2. By coming in with a nice slow waste pitch—just close enough to the plate to let the batter see it closely — you easily can ruin his timing enough to make him miss a fast pitch that comes right by him. The reverse can work just as effectively; by letting him see a fast pitch you can set him up for a change-up.

WORKING FAST/SLOW

Many sportswriters have been complaining that a baseball game takes too long. If that's true, why is the attendance at a doubleheader always larger than at a single game? At any rate, I'm sure I'm a favorite among those impatient writers because I like a fast-paced game. Games that I pitch usually take less than two hours. However, I still take my time between pitches if I think it's necessary. When I see a batter running to get up to the plate, I like to take a little extra time. If they're that anxious to hit, I don't think it hurts to make them wait an extra few seconds, and it just might make them edgy. So I stall a little by playing with my cap or adjusting my uniform until I'm ready. Another type of hitter takes

his time getting up to the plate. Cleon Jones is a principal offender; he really takes his time getting ready. So just to let him know who's boss I'll take a little extra time before I pitch. As for working faster than you usually do, I don't recommend it. When you start speeding up, you tend to get careless. But never hesitate to slow down when the situation demands it.

PITCHING OUT

The *pitchout* is your catcher's call. When he thinks the other team is going to steal or hit-and-run on a certain pitch, he'll call for a pitchout—a pitch that is thrown hard and straight and far enough away from the plate so that the batter cannot reach it even if he swings to protect the runner. However, it's up to you to put the ball in the right spot and make it easy for the catcher to make the play. If it works, a pitchout is baseball at its finest, and it takes a possible run away from your opponents. If it fails, the most it can cost you is a ball.

BRUSH BACK PITCH

When used correctly, the *brush back pitch* is an important part of good baseball strategy. When used incorrectly or by an untrained pitcher, it's a highly dangerous weapon. To brush back, or knock down, the hitter, you need to throw the pitch close enough to the hitter's body to make him move away from the plate. Often the brush back not only moves the hitter away from the plate but it also sends him sprawling to the ground. The brush back pitch is called for in only one situation: when a batter crowds the plate and digs in. There are many major leaguers—Ron Hunt, for instance—who get so close to the plate that they just challenge you to throw close. With Hunt it works: he holds the major league record for the number of times hit.

There is a second type of brush back pitch, known as the *beanball*. It is illegal—and stupid—to throw a beanball intentionally. A baseball is a substantial weapon when it is thrown at a speed approaching a hundred miles per hour. A beanball can do permanent damage to the person it hits. An intentional beanball usually is thrown behind the hitter's head rather than in front of it. This causes the hitter to duck into the ball when he tries to get out of the way.

In the major leagues you rarely see a true knockdown pitch. On most clubs there is a standing rule: if the opposing pitcher throws at a hitter in a situation that doesn't call for it, you must protect your teammates. Translated that means the first hitter up the next inning hits the dirt. (Although some managers say that since the pitcher threw the brush back, he's the player who should go down.)

Under no circumstances should you think about throwing a beanball. Unless you have excellent control, unless you're sure you can put every pitch where you want it every time, you shouldn't even throw a brush back pitch. I think Satchel Paige's advice is still good: "You can knock 'em down if you want to," he said, "but it don't do you no good. You still got to get 'em out."

PITCHING WITH A BIG LEAD

Many ballplayers on a winning team will tell you that they would rather be in a tight game than in a game that one team has blown wide open with a lot of runs. There is one thing you can say about people who make that statement: they're not pitchers. When you have a big lead, you can afford to be a little braver. With a big lead I'll challenge every hitter on the plate with fast balls. Remember that when a team is behind they'll be *taking* a lot of pitches because they need *base runners*. Most teams take a strike before swinging at the ball, and a good pitcher will take advantage of this to get ahead of the hitter. I never start grooving pitches, or throwing them right down the middle, though, and I never relax and let the other team hit the ball. I was beating the Mets 12-2 once, and I started getting careless. Three innings later the score was 12-8, and Jenkins was gone. When pitching with a substantial lead, keep the ball around the plate and throw strikes. Don't start laying the ball in there just to get the ball game over with.

THE CATCHER . . . is the mainstay of any team. He has to be intelligent
and have a good understanding of baseball strategy.

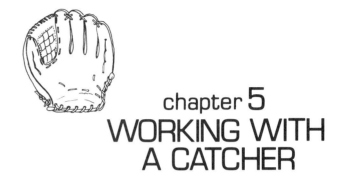

chapter 5
WORKING WITH A CATCHER

After having concluded a very successful major league career, pitcher Bobby Shantz told reporters, "I've never met a catcher I didn't look up to." Of course, the fact that Bobby was about 5'7" and had a big brother who was a catcher might have had something to do with his opinion. But I'm almost 6'5", and I still agree with Shantz: I have never met a catcher I didn't respect. Although it is the pitcher who gets the headlines, it's the catcher who is the mainstay of any team. He has to be intelligent; he has to have a good memory; and he has to have an excellent understanding of baseball strategy. The catcher is in charge of calling signals, moving players around, and setting the pace of the game as well as catching the ball.

A smart pitcher will work with his catcher right down the line. Before the game discuss what you'd like to do over the next nine innings, what pitches are working, and what hitters seem to hit you well. Above all make sure you know the signals. I really don't know why the pitcher-catcher combination is called the *battery,* but I expect it's because they are in "charge" of the team.

READING SIGNALS

A catcher and a pitcher must be able to communicate in every situation. Consequently, a baseball sign language has developed. This language covers almost every situation that can occur on the diamond. The Chicago Cubs have signals for every pitch, for *pick-offs* at every base, *cut-offs, pitchouts,* day and night signals, and what we call *flaps* (to be used with a runner on second). Most signals (Diagram 8) your catcher will give don't require any response — just execution. Your job is to recognize every sign immediately because games are lost when batteries fail to communicate. If you don't understand the signal your catcher is giving, call time and talk it over. Don't guess. If you are having trouble reading his signals, tell him so. He can tape the tops of his fingers, give signs higher on his leg to make them more visible, use closed and open fists rather than fingers—there is no limit to the different ways that he can communicate the signals. Use signals that are easy to see and simple to understand. Before every game sit down with your catcher and go over each and every one of them; discuss which set of signals will be used in certain situations.

PREGAME MEETINGS

The amount you accomplish during a pregame meeting goes a long way toward determining how much you will accomplish on the pitcher's mound. You and your catcher (and sometimes a coach) should decide exactly what you want to make happen on the field before every game. On the Cubs we review the pitching charts from previous games (see Chapter 4) and carefully discuss each batter: what pitch he hit last time, where he hit the pitch, and what the situation was. It really helps if you can identify the good clutch players who hit well in important situations. Then the catcher and I decide how we'll pitch each hitter and what we would like to make each one do. Major league catchers keep a close watch on box scores, and they can pick out the hot hitters—so we decide to pitch those hitters a little more carefully than usual. We review what to watch out for when the

hitters are on base: who likes to steal in various situations and whether he's getting his jump on the pitcher or catcher. Finally we review every signal.

I pitched to five different catchers in 1971, and I won 24 games. That doesn't mean I don't think catchers make a difference—I certainly do; what it does mean is that each catcher and I left the locker room in total agreement about what we would do on the field. By the time I ran out to the mound, I had total confidence in my catcher. Over the entire season I think I shook off fewer than a dozen pitches.

CONFERENCES ON THE MOUND

One of the best weapons in a catcher's arsenal is a stroll out to the pitcher's mound. He can come out for a visit for any number of reasons: if he wants to slow you down, to remind you of something ("This is the eighth hitter. We can pitch around him and get to the pitcher."), to check to see if you're tiring or starting to lose your stuff, to explain something he noticed about a batter, or to try to take your mind off the game. Sometimes I get into a negative train of thought and can't do anything right. A good catcher will talk to me about anything to get me to change my way of thinking.

You can use these conferences on the mound with your catcher to your advantage. When there is the slightest doubt in your mind about a signal, call out your catcher. When you think you've noticed something about a batter and would like to experiment, call out your catcher. When you need an extra 20 seconds of rest time to get your breath back, call him out.

HONESTY ON THE MOUND

Your day will come: your manager will walk slowly out to the mound and ask you how you feel. Are you tired? Is your stuff

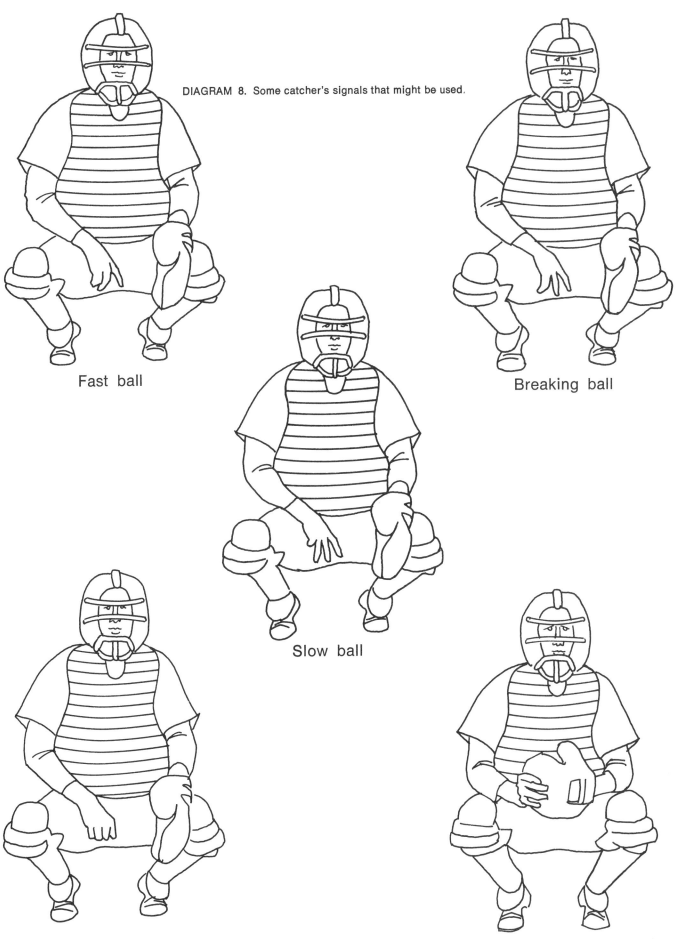

DIAGRAM 8. Some catcher's signals that might be used.

Fast ball

Breaking ball

Slow ball

Pitchout signal for the pitcher

Pitchout signal for an infielder

gone? Had enough? A pitcher with a lot of courage will stay out there and finish what he started. A pitcher with brains will tell the manager the truth. Getting tired is the most natural part of pitching. It's tough work, and it takes a lot out of you. Winning pitchers realize when they are tired, and when the manager wanders out, they are straight with him. No pitcher wants to be pulled from a game, but remember, baseball is a team effort, and you don't help anyone by trying to stay in the game one batter longer than you should. In fact, a smart pitcher will let his manager know as soon as he feels the slightest twinge of tiredness or when he feels that he is losing his stuff. Most managers will watch a pitcher carefully, and when the time comes for him to rest, he will have a relief pitcher ready to save the game.

SHAKING OFF A SIGNAL

Every once in a great while your catcher will signal for a pitch that you don't want to throw. If the catcher is adamant about it, he'll give you the same sign after you shake him off, and you probably will shake him off again. The batter may step out of the box, but there's no strategy involved here—just a natural disagreement between a pitcher and catcher. It happens. Occasions pop up during a game for which you have made no provision in your pregame meeting. The catcher may want a straight pitch when you don't want to throw it. Or you may have decided you have no confidence in your curve ball, or you simply don't feel like throwing a certain pitch. As I said before, pitching is a mental exercise, and if you don't have confidence in the pitch you're about to throw, don't throw it. Shake the catcher off and wait until he signals for the pitch you want to throw —then be ready to take the consequences.

I remember an incident in which I was pitching against Pete Rose with Chris Cannizarro as the catcher. Chris signaled for a fast ball inside, and I shook him off; I wanted to throw the slider. Finally we got together, and I threw the slider; it hung out right over the plate, and Rose put a line drive into the left field bleachers. The point of this story is that most of the time it pays to go along with your catcher.

WILD PITCHES AND PASSED BALLS

Your job is to throw the ball, and the catcher's job is to catch it. But sometimes he doesn't make the stop, and it may be your fault. Any pitch that gets by a catcher is classified as either a *wild pitch* or a *passed ball*. A wild pitch is one thrown so far out of the catcher's reach that he couldn't possibly catch it. On the other hand, a passed ball is a catcher's error, a playable pitch that the catcher misses.

A wild pitch is always your fault. The ball may have slipped out of your hand; you may have taken your eyes off the target; you might have been bothered by a base runner or a loud noise; you may have overstrained on the curve and put it in the dirt; or you may have slipped when you threw the ball. The list of reasons for making a wild pitch could go on and on. After you make a wild pitch, which should be infrequently, forget about it.

A passed ball can be the pitcher's fault as well as the catcher's. Very rarely does a catcher simply miss the ball; more often a passed ball is caused by a mix-up in signals. By not knowing the proper sign or by forgetting that the signals change with a man on second, you can easily cross up your catcher. Even though the official scorer calls it a passed ball, it is really your fault. A good example of a passed ball that was the pitcher's fault occurred in the 1941

World Series. Brooklyn Dodger pitcher Hugh Casey struck out Tommy Henrich of the Yankees for what should have been the final out. But the ball ticked off catcher Mickey Owen's mitt, and Henrich went to first. The Yankees, given a reprieve, came up with four runs and won the game. Owen had signaled for one pitch, but Casey had thrown another. Mickey Owen was blamed, but the error was really Casey's.

There is no hard rule about how to avoid wild pitches and passed balls. Concentration, confidence, and calmness are required, especially when players are on bases. When you do throw a pitch away, accept the fact without losing control of your pitches or your temper. There's absolutely nothing you can do about it.

ONCE YOU'VE RELEASED THE BALL . . . and it's speeding toward home plate, you may feel like relaxing. However, your pitching responsibilities are not over yet. There are areas of the field that you must cover and bases that have to be backed up.

chapter 6
PLAYING THE POSITION

On July 26, 1935, a right-handed player named Ed Linke was pitching for the Washington Senators. There were two out and a runner on second when the Yankees' Jesse Hill slammed a liner back at Linke. The ball hit Linke on the head and bounded back toward the plate, where catcher Jack Redmond caught the ball on a fly and instinctively threw to second base to finish the double play. Linke was hospitalized for three days, but he returned to win his next eight starts.

Once the ball leaves the pitcher's hand, he becomes the fifth *infielder*. You must be ready to field bunts and grounders, to start the double play, to call *pop-ups*, to cover first base, to back up the other bases, to position fielders, to hold runners on base, and to initiate the pick-off play. Any pitcher can be a good fielder if he works at it. *Fielding the position* is a matter of combining

good reflexes with anticipation. In other words, you have to know what you're going to do with the ball on every play and be able to do it. The anticipation comes from study and experience. Every year in spring training we get a book filled with diagrams showing us where to go in given situations. Then we practice those situations over and over. The first two weeks every spring we do nothing but cover first base, field bunts, and play pepper games. Nobody gripes because it is a fact of pitching life that a good fielding pitcher can help himself to win ball games.

FIELDING THE BUNT

The fielding play in which you will be involved most often is the *bunt*. As a pitcher your first job is to prevent the batter from actually laying the bunt down. The best way to do this is to keep the ball high and inside. With any luck the batter will pop the pitch straight up in the air. But if he is successful, if he does manage to lay the ball down, you become a vital part of the infield. On any bunt play you may end up fielding the ball, covering a base, or tagging a runner. Your area of responsibility on bunts is shown in Diagram 9.

The best way to set yourself up for a bunt play is to recognize a possible bunt situation. There are three different types of bunts—the sacrifice, suicide, and base hit—and each calls for a different reaction from you.

The Sacrifice Bunt

A *sacrifice bunt* is used to advance the base runner at the expense of the bunter, and the object is to put the runner in a scoring position. Normally the sacrifice bunt is used in a close game, with a man on first, less than two outs, and a reasonably weak hitter at bat or a strong batter due up next. A well-placed sacrifice bunt will force the pitcher or the first baseman rather than the third baseman to field the ball, because the third baseman can field the ball and throw to second in one motion, while the pitcher and first baseman must take time to turn before

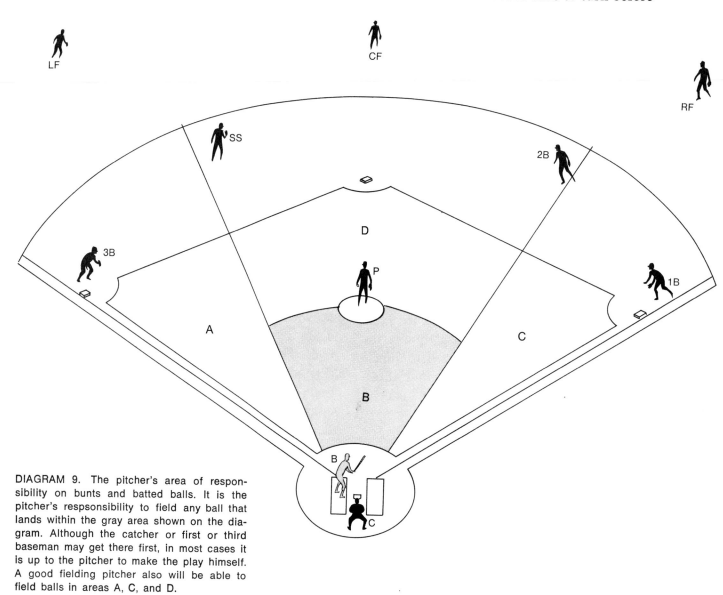

DIAGRAM 9. The pitcher's area of responsibility on bunts and batted balls. It is the pitcher's respsonsibility to field any ball that lands within the gray area shown on the diagram. Although the catcher or first or third baseman may get there first, in most cases it is up to the pitcher to make the play himself. A good fielding pitcher also will be able to field balls in areas A, C, and D.

they can throw. On the Cubs the catcher will call the play: if he can field it, he'll take it; if he can't, he'll holler to the player who should and indicate what base that player should throw to.

If the pitcher fields the ball, his play will usually be to first base (Diagram 10). After taking a quick look at second, the pitcher's throw should be high and to the inside part of first base so that it won't hit the runner. If the bunt is up the first base line and the first baseman must field the ball, it's up to the pitcher—or the second baseman—to cover the base. If you cover first, catch the ball just as you reach the base and get off the base as quickly as possible. A bunt up the first base line is a play we go over a thousand times in practice.

If a bunt is hit down the third base line, the third baseman may make the play. It's up to the pitcher to make sure someone is covering third. If the shortstop is not there, the pitcher should cover. Remember, most plays to third are not force plays, and the runner must be tagged.

A sacrifice bunt situation usually is quite obvious. Be ready to get off the mound quickly and try to anticipate your play. Usually your instinct—and a few years of practice—will tell you whether you go for the ball or the base.

The Suicide Bunt

There are two types of *suicide bunts*: the *squeeze play* and the *safety squeeze*. A suicide situation arises in a close game with a man on third (at least), a right-handed hitter at bat (to block the catcher's view), and less than two out. If the runner breaks for the plate with the pitch, the suicide squeeze is on. If the batter bunts the ball, the runner will score; if he misses, the runner probably will be out.

The safety squeeze is more like the sacrifice bunt: the runner waits off third until the ball is safely on the ground; then he breaks toward the plate. Although normal bunt situations call for you to keep the ball high and tight, when you see a runner break for the plate, you must get the hitter out of the way and prevent him from bunting. The best way is to throw right at the hitter's shoulder. To protect himself he will have to fall out of the way, putting your catcher in a perfect position to make the play. However, if the hitter does manage to get the ball down, you have to trust your instincts. If you feel you have a chance to get the runner at the plate, make the play. Otherwise straighten up and throw to the inside of first base. If the safety squeeze is on and you field the ball, the first thing you do is look at third base (this is known as "looking the runner back to the base"), and make your play to first (Diagram 11). One thing to be careful of with a bunt to the left side of the infield is colliding with the third baseman. He will usually be charging in to make the play; it will be easier for him to make the play than it would be for you. When someone else is fielding the ball you must make sure that every base is covered.

Base Hit

There is no obvious situation in which a batter will try to bunt for a *base hit*, although good hitters in prolonged batting slumps often try to bunt their way out of them. Mickey Mantle, who had very few slumps, was one of the bunting masters of modern baseball. As a left-handed batter, Mantle would take his first step toward first base as the pitcher released the ball, so as he bunted—or dragged the ball—he was already on his way to the base. When bunting for a base hit you try to make the second baseman or shortstop field the ball.

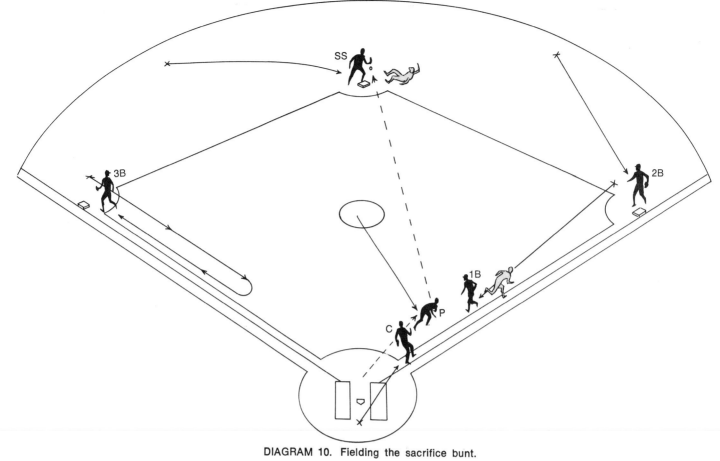

DIAGRAM 10. Fielding the sacrifice bunt.

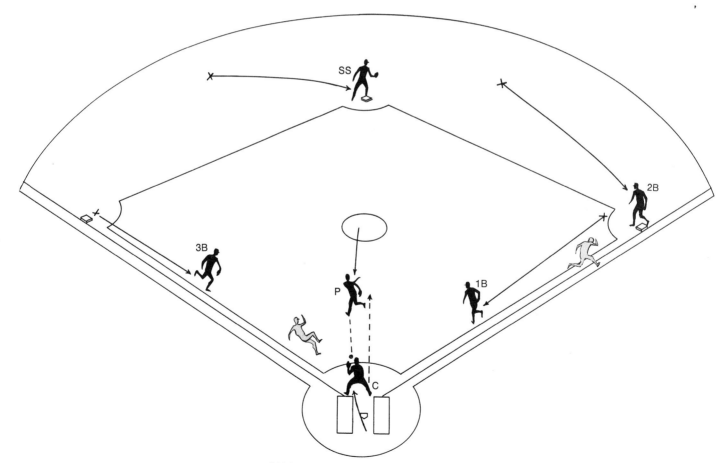

DIAGRAM 11. The suicide squeeze.

To do this the hitter must bunt hard and place the ball carefully between the pitcher and the first or third baseman. If a pitcher's reaction time is good and he starts moving in the right direction as soon as the hitter "shortens" to bunt, he can make the play. Bob Gibson is excellent at getting off the mound quickly on this type of play. If the bunter is good, there is little you can do except keep him from stealing second.

COVERING FIRST

I very rarely see a young player cover first base on ground balls to the right side of the infield. Covering ground balls to the right side of the infield is the responsibility of the pitcher; yet even players in the majors occasionally fail to do this. On every ball hit to the right side you automatically should break to cover first base (Diagram 12). If the first baseman has to field the ball, it is up to you to make the play, and unless you break as soon as the ball is hit, you'll never beat the runner. Another part of your responsibility is to cover first when the first baseman has taken himself out of the play by going after the ball, even if the second baseman has picked it up. I have to admit that I sometimes fail to cover first base. Burned indelibly into my mind is a scene in which first baseman Joe Pepitone knocked down a grounder and then stood there helplessly, waiting to flip the ball to me as I watched entranced from the mound.

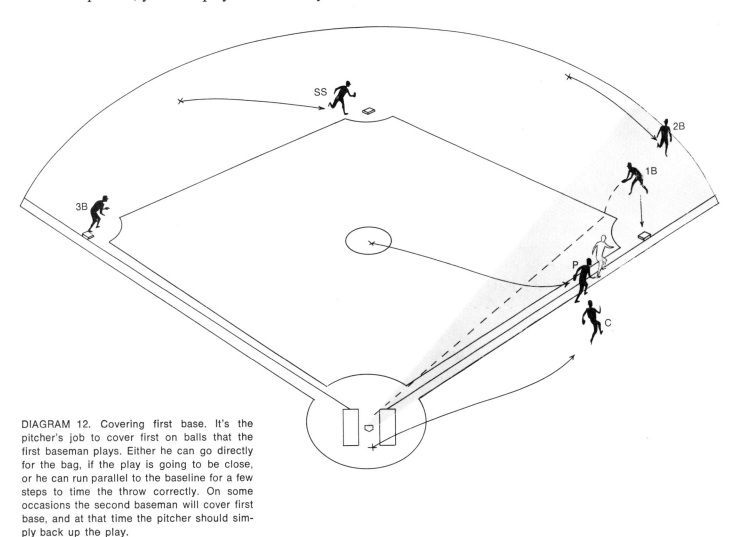

DIAGRAM 12. Covering first base. It's the pitcher's job to cover first on balls that the first baseman plays. Either he can go directly for the bag, if the play is going to be close, or he can run parallel to the baseline for a few steps to time the throw correctly. On some occasions the second baseman will cover first base, and at that time the pitcher should simply back up the play.

PICK-OFF AT FIRST BASE. My procedure for picking a runner off at first base is shown in the next four photos (*from left to right*). In the first photo I look toward the base, receiving the signal from the first baseman. In the second photo I bring the ball and glove up, and then in one continuous motion I push off with my right foot (*third photo*), plant my left foot, and make the throw (*fourth photo*).

PICKING OFF

I have my own name for the pick-off play. I call it "pitcher-magic" because when it works, it makes base runners disappear. No matter how good a pitcher you are, every few innings someone is going to get on base. When that happens, your task is to make it as tough as possible for him to advance to the next base, and the best way to do that is to hold him as close as possible to the base he occupies. If a runner can't get a good lead, he probably won't try to steal, and you will have a better chance of forcing him on a bunt play or starting a double play.

The threat of the pick-off is just as important as the actual pick-off move. By throwing over to the base once or twice you remind the runner that you can make a move to pick him off, and that threat is usually enough to keep him honest. Of course, every once in a while you will want to attempt to catch the runner as he leans the wrong way. With great runners such as Lou Brock or Maury Wills you usually have a good shot at picking them off because their thoughts are centered on getting to the next base, not getting back to the base they started on.

I start my pick-off move to all bases in exactly the same way. I take a stretch position, my feet straddling the pitching rubber, and I lean in to take the sign from the catcher. Then I come to a set position. I check all runners the same, with a simple swivel of my head. But the actual move of picking them off requires a different action for each base.

First Base

For a left-handed pitcher a pick-off to first base is the easiest move; however, for the right-handed pitcher it takes a bit of practice. For either pitcher it is normally the first baseman who will initiate the play by giving the go-ahead sign. On our club the first baseman shows an open glove or

yawns as a go-ahead sign for picking off the runner on first base. There is no acknowledgment sign required from the pitcher because the first baseman usually is right in position, holding the runner on the base. To pick off the runner on first base the left-handed pitcher simply steps in the direction of first base and flips the ball over to the first baseman. The right-handed pitcher must, in one continuous motion, push off with his right foot, plant his left, and make the throw (Diagram 13). The throw itself should be a wrist flip rather than a full blown windup because speed counts, and you can't spare the time for a windup. The ball should be aimed low and to the inside of the base so that the first baseman can catch the ball and make the tag all in one motion.

Second Base

The pick-off move to second base is one of the most difficult plays to execute properly because it requires perfect timing on the part of the pitcher and either the second baseman or shortstop—whoever is covering the base. The pick-off play to second base is started on a sign from whoever is covering the base; he may touch his cap, call my last name, or show me an open glove. I acknowledge the fact that I've received the sign by touching the back of my neck. I take my stretch position, and the moment I come to my belt, in the set position, both the fielder and I begin counting silently: one one-thousand, two one-thousand, three one-thousand. At the two count the fielder breaks to the bag; at three I take one short step back with my right foot, whirl, and flip to the base (Diagram 14). Ideally, the ball and fielder arrive at the same time, an instant before the runner.

The throw to second base should be low and to the third base side of the bag. This is a tough play because you have to start throwing while you're still spinning, and too often the ball ends up sailing into center field. One important thing to remember

DIAGRAM 13. The pitcher's view of a first base pick-off.

DIAGRAM 14. Picking off on second for a right-handed pitcher.

2nd Base

about the pick-off to second is that, unlike making a move to first or third, baseball rules permit you to turn to the base without actually throwing the ball. So even if the play isn't on, if you think the runner is too far off the bag, it's a good idea to go through the motions of a pick-off move, just to let him know you haven't forgotten he's there.

Third Base

Throwing to third base is just the opposite of throwing to first: for a right-handed pitcher it's easy; for a left-handed pitcher it's tough. Right-handed pitchers simply take one step toward the base, plant their foot, and throw to the base. You rarely see a runner picked off third because the third baseman usually doesn't stay on the base, as the first baseman does. Also, if you throw the ball away, you're giving up a run. Ron Santo usually takes care of our third base problems by bluffing the runner back to the bag. If there is a play, it is called by the third baseman. There is no count; Ron simply breaks to the bag, and it's up to the pitcher to get the ball there. The throw to third base should be low and to the home plate side of the bag.

BALKING

After you have decided that you are going to try to pick the runner off base, you must go through with it—except to second, as was mentioned previously. If you don't go through with the pick-off, it is considered a *balk,* and every runner on base is entitled to move up to the next base. A balk is defined completely in rule 8.05 of the baseball rules, but the main points are worth explaining here in relation to your pick-off move. It is a balk if you do any of the following: stand on the pitching rubber, make a motion to throw to home plate and do not complete the throw; make a move to throw to first and then not throw the ball; make a motion to throw to a base or home plate without the ball — when trying the hidden ball trick, for example; pitch without having your foot on the pitching rubber; pitch from a stretch position without coming to a full stop in the set position.

To prevent balks begin by knowing the rules. The next step is to practice the proper way to pick off runners without balking. Every day in the early part of the year you should practice your move to all the bases until it becomes natural and fluid. It takes time to develop an effective pick-off move, and even when you have it down pat, you don't eliminate the possibility of balking.

My worst year for committing balks was in 1971, when I balked three different times. Pitching against Houston I had started my pick-off motion when I heard their third base coach yelling something to the runner. Instinctively I looked toward third, and I was called for a balk. The runner was waved to second, and he eventually came around to score the winning run. My second balk of 1971 also was against Houston; this time it was in Chicago. I turned to check the runner on second and knocked my cap off and stopped my motion. That's a balk. The third balk was against Shortstop Larry Bawa of the Philadelphia Phillies in Chicago. I saw the runner on first take a big lead, and instead of going through my regular pick-off motion—step, plant, throw—I neglected to take my right foot off the rubber before I threw to first. Because I threw to first without directing my intention there, the umpire accurately called balk number three. Almost anything out of the ordinary can make you balk if it breaks your concentration. There is no way to eliminate balks, but the more you concentrate on what you want to do, the less often you'll do the wrong thing.

BACKING UP THE BASES

Whenever there is a possibility of a play at third base or home plate, you should be ready to back it up. Backing up a play is easy in terms of execution; it is simply a matter of putting your body in the right place. But many pitchers forget to do it because they are too busy standing on the mound thinking about the bad pitch they threw. Forget the bad pitch. After the batter hits the ball, you're a fielder.

To back up third base (Diagram 15) line yourself up with the angle of the throw and the third baseman and stand about 20 feet behind the base. If the ball is overthrown or underthrown and gets by the third baseman, you not only can prevent the runner on third from walking home, but you can prevent every other runner on base from advancing and getting you in even worse trouble.

It is important to back up the plate whenever there will be a play there. Line yourself up with the *cut-off man* and the catcher (or the throw and the catcher, depending on how good the throw is). Although you might not be able to do anything about stopping a run, you can prevent other runners from advancing on a bad throw.

STARTING THE DOUBLE PLAY

One of the most important plays for a pitcher to be able to execute properly is the pitcher-to-second-to-first double play (Diagram 16). And like most play-action movements in baseball, the proper execution of the double play begins in practice. Get one of your teammates to hit ground balls back to you in the vicinity of the pitcher's mound; practice wheeling, getting set, and making accurate, quick throws to second base. You should practice the double play move so often that it becomes a natural movement.

During the game you must realize when the possibility of a double play exists. Be-

fore I throw every pitch, I always ask myself, "If the ball is hit back to me, what am I going to do with it?" Then I stick to the decision I make at that moment. There is a possibility of a double play when there is a man on first and fewer than two outs. If a right-handed hitter is at bat, the second baseman should cover second; if the batter is left-handed, the shortstop should make the play. (To cross up a hitter with great bat control and to take away the chance of a *hit-and-run play,* we switch around our cover assignments every so often.) The infielder that will be covering the base should give you a sign. After you field the ball, set yourself up so that you can make an accurate throw. Managers always remind you to "make sure of one," and they're right. If you try to throw too quickly, the ball will end up in the outfield, and you'll be backing up home plate. The throw should be hard and lead the fielder across the base so that he can catch the ball and make the play to first in one motion.

HOLDING RUNNERS ON BASE

The first thing you do when the ball is hit back to you with men on base—and the possibility of a double play does not exist—is to check the lead runner. Look directly at him, and if he doesn't start to return to his base, raise your arm to throw. The runner is usually watching your arm, and when you cock it, he'll get back. If he doesn't, you may have a play on him. When the ball is hit back to the mound, you usually have plenty of time to check the runner and make the play. But don't waste time. If you move too slowly, you won't get the runner at first.

RUN-DOWNS

Sometimes the ball will be hit back to you, and you will turn and catch the runner between two bases (Diagram 17). If he keeps

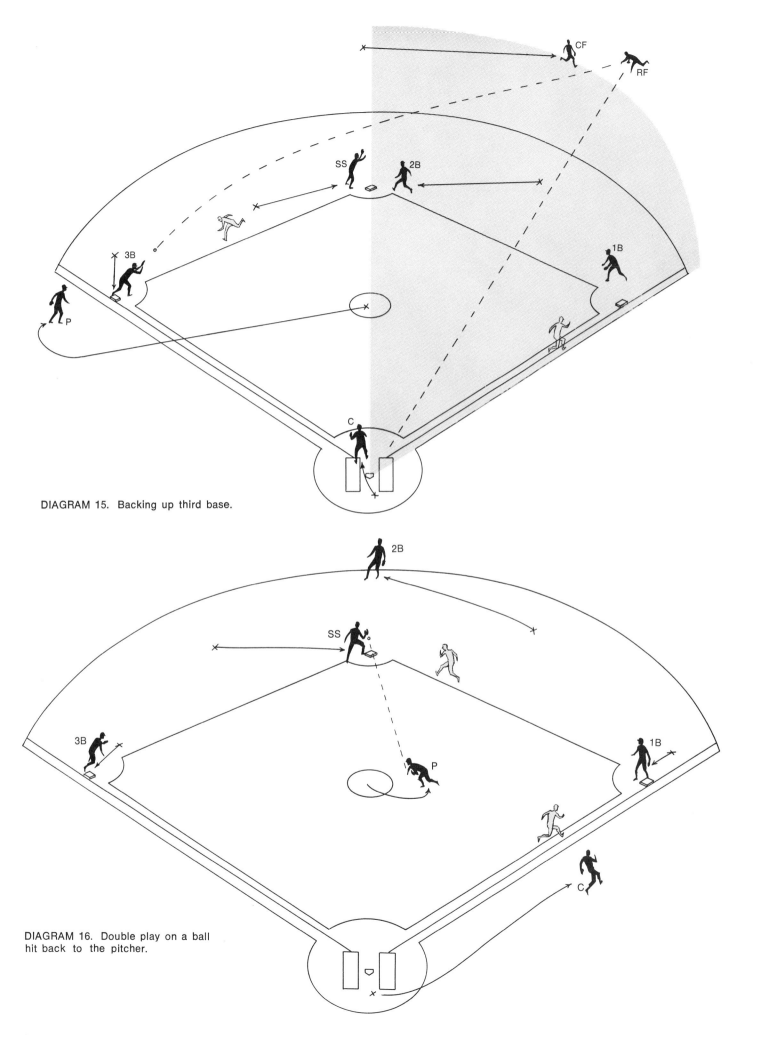

DIAGRAM 15. Backing up third base.

DIAGRAM 16. Double play on a ball hit back to the pitcher.

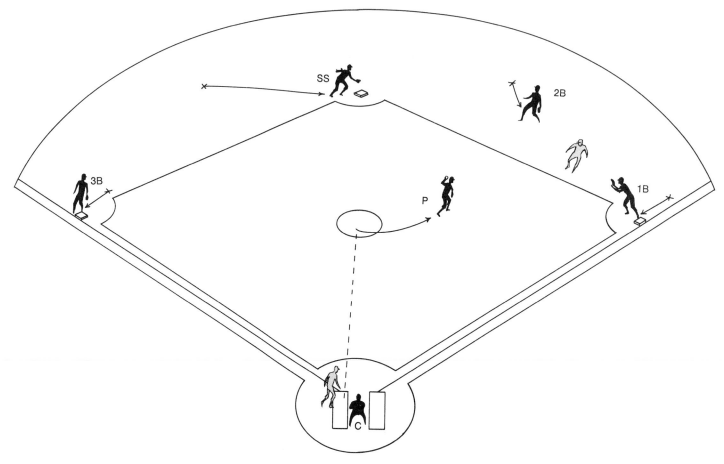

DIAGRAM 17. Catching a runner off base.

running, throw the ball to the base that he is going to. However, most often he'll stop and try to make you commit yourself by throwing to a base. Don't throw; run right at him. The object is to make him commit himself. You can hope that he will go back to the base that he started from so that if he escapes the *run-down,* at least he will not have advanced. As soon as the runner is caught in the run-down, flip the ball to the infielder nearest him and cover the advance base. A well-executed run-down will get the runner out in two throws.

Your responsibility in every run-down, even the ones you don't start, is to make sure there is a fielder covering every base. If there is, be prepared to back them up in case of an overthrow. On run-downs between first and second base I will usually cover first; on run-downs between second

and third, I will cover third; between third and home I will cover the plate.

TAG PLAYS

On occasion, the pitcher has to make the *tag* himself. Most often you will have to make the tag when you're covering a base during a run-down. Begin by having the ball securely in your glove. If the runner is standing up, hold the ball with both hands so that he can't jar it out of your glove. If he is coming in on a slide, get your pitching hand out of the way or you'll get it spiked. Hold the glove with the ball in it between the base and the man and let him slide into the glove.

MOVING PLAYERS AROUND

The way in which you are going to pitch to a particular hitter determines where your fielders should be playing. It is usually up to the catcher, the manager, and the coaches to position players, but I always check my fielders before I throw the first pitch to a hitter. If I see someone playing in a poor position for the way I intend to pitch to the batter, I'll move him. I *know* where I want the batter to hit the ball, so I try to have the fielders covering those areas.

RESPONSIBILITY ON POP-UPS

When a ball is popped up in the infield, the pitcher becomes the director of the action. Because it is quite easy to lose your balance coming off the mound, pitchers rarely catch pop-ups. However, it is your job to call out the infielder who should make the play and to ward off collisions by calling off any other fielders who may be attempting to catch the ball. When there is a pop-up near the stands, you should shout instructions to the fielder about how close he is to the wall and the dugout. On pop-ups behind the catcher you should tell him where the ball is until he can spot it himself.

PITCHERS ARE USUALLY THE WEAKEST HITTERS . . . on a team, because they don't have as much of a chance to practice their hitting as do the other members of a team. However, as a pitcher you should know how to hit and to hit well, because you can save your team many ball games by doing what is expected of you when you come up to the plate.

Reprinted with permission from the Chicago Sun-Times; Photo by Bob Langer

chapter 7
BATTING AND BASE RUNNING

The pitcher always bats ninth because there are only 9 players allowed in the batting lineup. I have no doubt that if all 25 men on a big league roster were allowed to bat, the pitching staff would occupy spaces 18-25. With few exceptions, pitchers are by far the worst hitters in baseball. For example, Sandy Koufax came to bat 12 times in his rookie year and struck out every time. There are legitimate reasons why pitchers can't hit: they have very little time to practice batting, and they don't get to the plate as often as the other players. Another big reason is a mental excuse—pitchers have long been told that they can't hit and that they aren't supposed to be able to hit, so they don't work at it. To me that doesn't make any sense. If a manager knows you can put the bat on the ball, that you might

get on base or advance the runner, that you probably won't strike out, then you will stay in a lot of close ball games and pick up a few extra victories every year.

Not every pitcher is a strikeout artist at bat. The Dodgers used Don Drysdale to *pinch hit* at times; the Yankees did the same with Tommy Byrne, and I won't be surprised if I eventually do some pinch hitting. Right now many people consider me one of the best hitting pitchers in baseball. As far as I know, I have hit more home runs than any other active pitcher. The reason for this is that I work at my hitting. I didn't start pitching until I was 16 years old, and by then I had a basic idea of how to swing a bat. When I'm in the *batter's box,* I put my pitching knowledge to work. I think, if I were the pitcher, what would I throw to me? Then when the ball is pitched I take a nice, easy, level swing. I don't try to kill the ball. As Ted Williams advised, I try to hit everything to center field. And for confidence I keep remembering a left-handed pitcher named George Herman "Babe" Ruth.

Once you get on base, you have to know what to do. *Stealing, sliding,* and *tagging up* are important aspects of baseball strategy, and you can help yourself as well as the team by being proficient in all offensive aspects of the game.

READING SIGNS

Pitchers are not always expected to get a hit when they bat. More often they are expected to bunt a base runner along, to draw a walk, or to cover an attempted steal. The third base coach gives you your orders through a series of signals (Diagram 18). If you are going to be given a sign, there usually will be some prior indication. The third base coach may touch his hat or wipe his hands across his letters — this means you had better pay attention because something is expected of you. Then he will give you the actual sign. It may be the take sign (don't swing at the next pitch), the bunt sign, or the signal to hit and run. (Because pitchers don't ordinarily hit well, runners often will try to steal with the pitcher at bat. The pitcher is expected to swing the bat to cover him.) It's your job to carry out the orders given to you by the coach, no matter where the pitch is.

The only sign that you have to answer when you come up to bat is the suicide squeeze. When the coach gives you the suicide squeeze sign, it means the runner is going to try to score on the next pitch, and you'd better protect him. You should answer the coach with another signal to be certain that you and the coach understand each other.

Reading signs is vitally important. Make sure that you know your team's offensive signals. If the situation calls for a specific play and you haven't picked up the sign, call time out and ask the third base coach what play he is calling. If you think you may have misunderstood a signal, ask the coach. Review every offensive signal before you step out on the field.

There is a whole set of signals used for base runners. If you should get on base, keep a sharp eye on the third base coach. Unless there is a man on base ahead of you, you probably won't get the steal sign. But many managers like to play hit-and-run with the pitcher on base. Do yourself a favor and know every sign.

BUNTING

It is generally agreed that pitchers are not expected to be good hitters, but they do have to be excellent bunters. The bunt is the pitcher's primary offensive weapon. He uses it to advance a man into scoring position or to move a player to third so that he can score on a later sacrifice fly. The pitcher must be the best bunter in the lineup because when he is at bat, there are often runners on bases, and the bunt is expected.

On the Cubs we begin bunting the first day of spring training. We take a minimum of ten minutes of bunting practice in the batting cages and then play pepper games. Every day for the entire season we bunt in pregame practice. The art of bunting is a precise one; it is more than just putting the bat on the ball. Before you hit the ball, you must decide where you want to place it.

If there is a runner on first base, the first baseman will usually come charging in on a bunt. If the first baseman is left-handed, you need to keep the ball away from him

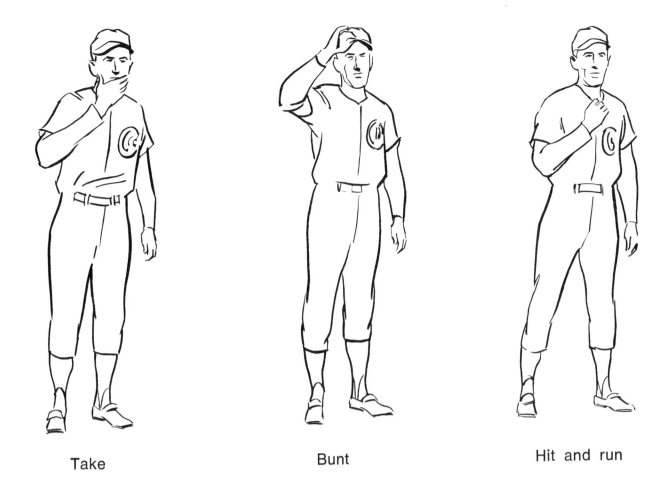

Take   Bunt   Hit and run

DIAGRAM 18. Some of the possible signals used by the third base coach when the pitcher is hitting.

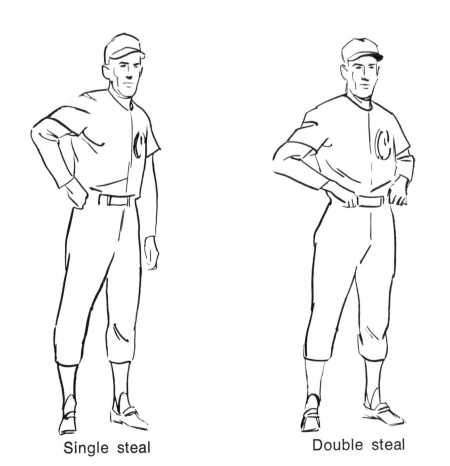

Single steal   Double steal   Running squeeze play

BUNTING. On the Cubs we hold the bat diagonally in most bunting situations; the barrel is held about shoulder height, and the handle is held down at waist level.

There are two schools of thought about the proper method of bunting. Some teams teach their players to hold the bat level and move it from side to side. On the Cubs we hold the bat diagonally; the barrel, or thick part of the bat, is held about shoulder height, and the handle is held down at waist level. It's easier to move the bat up and down than from side to side. When you bunt right-handed, your right hand should be on the barrel of the bat and your left hand on the handle (left-handed players do the reverse). The farther up on the bat that your right hand is, the easier it is to deaden the ball — to make it stop just a few feet in front of home plate. The top of the bat handle should be moved up to about shoulder level when you meet the ball. You should not have to reach up to bunt — anything above your shoulders will be a ball anyway. When you grip the bat, don't wrap your right hand around the barrel. If you do, you're likely to end up with a few broken fingers. The bat should be cradled between the thumb and the forefinger and held just above the label of the bat.

As the pitch comes in start shifting your body weight until you have brought your back foot parallel to your front foot and you're facing the pitcher directly. If you're bunting down the first base line, your hands should be out and extended over home plate. If you're bunting toward third, your left hand is pulled back into your body, and the bat is held almost vertical.

When you are up in a bunting situation, I suggest you use a bat with a barrel that is a little thicker than you normally would use. The bigger the barrel, the more surface you have to bunt with. And the better the bunt, the more chance you have of staying in the game. Bunting is a pitcher's medium. I've won quite a few games because I've been able to move a man into scoring position in a bunting situation.

because he can pick it up and throw it to second in one motion. If the first baseman is right-handed, he will have to take some time to turn before he can throw. Ideally, you force the pitcher to field the ball. If there is a runner on second base, you need to bunt the ball in such a way that the third baseman will have to field the ball; consequently, he will vacate the bag.

ALTHOUGH PITCHERS . . . are not expected to be particularly good hitters, they do have to be good bunters. Here I have the barrel of the bat positioned to meet the ball as it starts to come in. *Reprinted with permission from the* Chicago Sun-Times; *Photo by Bob Langer*

SWINGING AWAY

There are times when you will come to bat in a nonbunting situation: no one on base, or a man on third, or men on base with two outs. If you have spent a lot of extra time in the batting cage or if you have a good natural eye, this is the spot in which you can do yourself the most good. I won the Cy Young Award as the best pitcher in the National League in 1971, and part of the reason for my receiving the award is that 1971 was my most productive year at the plate. I won a total of 24 games pitching, and in 8 of those games I knocked in the winning run. For example, against Montreal I had 2 home runs in one game. In another 1971 game I had a triple, a double, and 4 runs batted in to beat Atlanta. I batted in a total of 22 runs for the year. I go to the plate with two thoughts in mind: make contact with the ball and don't strike out. If you hit the ball, there is a reasonable chance it will go through for a hit. As a

WHEN I STEP UP TO THE PLATE . . . (*four photos from left to right*), I take a comfortable, natural stance; my feet are spread, and I don't take much of a crouch (*first photo*). As the pitch is delivered (*second photo*), I shift my weight to my rear foot, stride forward into the pitch, and start bringing the bat around (*third photo*). Then, with all my power, I swing through (*fourth photo*).

pitcher I don't like Ted Williams's suggestion that everything should be hit up the middle, but as a batter I follow it carefully. When I play pepper games, I hold the bat by the handle and try to hit everything directly back to the person who threw it. This is the best practice for meeting the ball and hitting it where it is pitched.

I set myself for a pitch by taking a comfortable, natural stance. My feet are spread, and I don't take much of a crouch. As the pitch is delivered, I shift my weight to my rear foot and stride forward, into the pitch, with my front foot. I never take my eyes off the ball; I try to keep my swing as level as possible and follow through completely. The object of swinging at the ball is to meet it.

I like to use one of the bigger barreled bats when I'm swinging away for the same reason that I like to use a big bat when I'm bunting — the more surface area I have, the easier it is to make contact with the ball.

BASE RUNNING

Not only did I win eight games as a hitter in 1971, but I also scored the winning run in two other games. If you should get on base, the objects are to not get picked off and to be ready to run. Some pitchers are excellent base runners. The Mets often use Tom Seaver as a *pinch runner* because he really thinks when he is out on a base. When you are on base, you know and the pitcher out on the mound knows that you're not going to try to steal; consequently, he's not going to hold you on base too tightly. When running bases take a good safe *lead* before the pitch, and as the pitcher moves toward the plate, lean toward the base you're heading for and take a step in that

direction. A good, safe lead is usually three to four strides, far enough to get a decent jump on the ball but close enough to get back if the pitcher decides to throw over. If the batter takes the pitch, go all the way back to the base and retouch. And don't get off the base until the pitcher has stepped back onto the rubber.

BASE STEALING

In rare circumstances you will have the opportunity to steal a base. When the opportunity presents itself, take advantage of it. If you are on base and the pitcher, having forgotten about you, begins to take a full windup, take off. By the time the ball reaches the plate, you'll be standing safely on the next base. Also, if you're on first and there's a man on third with two out your manager might want to send you down. If

the catcher chooses not to risk letting that man from third come home and doesn't make a play on you, you've stolen a base. If the catcher does throw to second and you see that you can't make it safely, your job is to get caught in a run-down and stay in that run-down long enough for the man from third to score. You won't have many opportunities to steal a base, but be ready to go at all times.

RUN–DOWNS

There is only one suggestion I can make to help you if you are caught in a run-down — try to get out of it. When you are caught between two bases, there is little you can do except to try to draw as many throws as possible. By doing so you give other runners on base the opportunity to advance. Also there is always the chance that one of the fielders will make a bad throw. If you are in a run-down and you see a fielder standing on the base line without the ball, run right into him. The umpire will call interference on him, and you will be awarded the base you were going to.

SLIDING

A pitcher is often called upon to *slide,* and unless he knows what he's doing he is liable to get hurt. When a play is going to be close, it is better to slide into base than to go in standing up because by sliding you make it tougher for the fielder to make the tag.

We start sliding practice early in spring training and do most of our work on grass. We wear canvas sliding pants, but you can substitute a pair of bermuda shorts and get almost the same protection. There is one important rule to remember about sliding: when you make up your mind to slide, *slide!* The easiest way to get hurt is to change your mind in mid-slide or to go into the base half-sliding and half-standing.

When you are on base, it is a good idea to bend down and pick up some dirt in your fists. That way, if you have to slide, you will naturally keep your hands off the ground and prevent possible cuts and bruises.

SLIDING. As a pitcher you can use any type of slide you want to except the dive slide. Remember, you have to protect your investment. Sometimes getting to that base in time is more difficult than it looks. *Reprinted with permission from the* Chicago Sun-Times; *Photo by Joe Kordick*

If you're on first and the batter hits a grounder to the infield, you'll be called upon to "take out" the shortstop or the second baseman, whichever player is covering second base. The object is to prevent the completion of the double play by sliding right into him, even if he is not standing on the base. If you don't hold back when you do take a player out, chances are that neither you nor the player you are taking out will get hurt. Injuries usually occur when you try to make unnatural moves.

There are three basic slides: the *straight,* the *hook,* and the *dive.* The best slide is the straight slide (Diagram 19) because it is the fastest and safest way of sliding into a base. You begin your straight slide when you're between 10 and 15 feet from the base. You slide with your bottom leg tucked underneath your body and your top leg extended straight out. Your back should be facing the direction that the ball is coming from. You aim for the middle of the base and hit it with your outstretched top leg. As you hit the base, your leg should give and let your body slide into the bag.

DIAGRAM 19. Straight slide.

DIAGRAM 20. Hook slide.

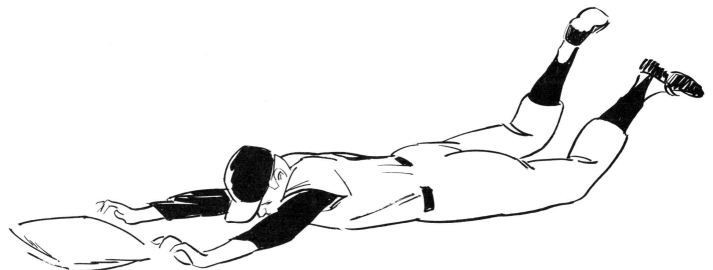

DIAGRAM 21. Dive slide.

The hook slide (Diagram 20) is used when the fielder has the ball and is ready to make the tag. To avoid being tagged you actually slide past the base and try to hook it as you go by with either your bottom, bent leg or your arm.

In a dive (Diagram 21) you make a leap for the base with your arms and hands stretched out in front of you. I don't think that a pitcher should dive, because he can easily jam his thumb or injure his pitching hand.

Sliding is quite easy and natural once you have practiced a few times. But remember, don't change your mind in mid-slide.

TAGGING UP

If you're on second or third base and the batter hits a fly ball, you can tag up and advance to the next base after the catch. The most important thing to remember in tagging up is not to leave your base until the ball has been caught. Whenever you are in a possible tag-up situation, check the outfielders to see where they are playing. It helps you to know which outfielders have good arms and which do not. When the ball is hit, take one look and then get ready to run. If you're on second, watch your third base coach. As soon as the ball is caught in the outfield, he will signal you to start taking off. If you're on third when the ball is caught, the third base coach will yell for you to go ahead. When he does, start running. If you try to watch for the ball to be caught, you are going to lose some time and possibly cost your team a run.

ALTHOUGH CONDITIONING . . . is probably the most unpleasant aspect of being a pitcher, it is probably one of the most important parts of your training. You can have all the pitching ability in the world, but if you get tired and your arm konks out, you won't last through another inning.

chapter 8
KEEP YOURSELF IN SHAPE

In the major leagues it is widely known that some hurlers are six-inning pitchers. This means that for the first six or seven innings, they are as tough as anyone around, but after that they lose their control or their speed and have nothing left for the last few innings of the game. The reason some pitchers fall apart is that they have not taken proper care of their bodies in general and their arms in particular. This chapter very well may be the most important one in the book, since it deals with conditioning your body.

The pitcher should always be the strongest person on a baseball team. Pitching demands things from your body that no other position requires. Every fourth day you are using your arm, your legs, shoulders, and hips to the full extent of their capabilities. I have played other sports — hockey, track, and basketball — and nothing takes as much out of me as pitching nine innings of baseball. As a working definition, conditioning is a matter of being able to carry out physically what you demand from your body. Knowing what to do or how to do it isn't worth anything if you don't have enough stamina to follow through or if your arm is too sore to proceed.

Conditioning is the most unpleasant part of baseball. There are no fans around to cheer you on, no one jotting down statistics. Often exercises are long and boring, and you have no scale with which you can compare yourself. You can't tell by looking in a mirror if you're in condition — Mickey Lolich has a potbelly, but it hasn't stopped him from being one of baseball's finest pitchers. Mickey knows exactly what his body requires. The only time your condition will be tested is when you are on the pitcher's mound. You'll be pitching in the last innings on a very hot day; you'll reach back for that little extra speed for the fast ball, and that's the moment you'll know whether or not you are in condition.

DURING THE SEASON—YOUR BODY

General conditioning exercises are designed to build both strength and stamina. A good in-season conditioning program begins the very first day of preseason practice. After an extended layoff your muscles are tight and probably flabby. Using the basic exercises explained on the following pages, start to work your body into shape very slowly. Don't try to do too much in one day because tight and underconditioned muscles can cause injuries, and injuries will put you more out of condition than you were originally. Once you've managed to put your body into acceptable shape, you have to continue to exercise throughout the entire season. As the season progresses, your body will become more tired, and exercising will become even more important. The basic pitching exercises vary according to your individual needs, but I stick to the few that have worked best for my body.

Loosening-up Exercises

Before you do anything else, you must loosen up your muscles. Every day during the season I go through an entire series of these exercises as soon as I get out on the field. I'll start by doing some basic toe-touching exercises. I spread my legs apart, bend from my waist, and touch my toes. First I reach my right hand to my left foot and then my left hand to my right foot. Next I do some body-benders by putting my hands on my hips and twisting as far to the right as I can without moving my feet. Then I twist to the left and bend over, straighten my back, and finally bend forward. After the body-benders I do some

simple leg-stretchers. To do a leg-stretcher properly, take one step to the right, bend your knee, and put all your weight on that leg. Then take a step to the left and do the same thing. The last of the loosening-up exercises is the old deep knee bend. Put your hands on your hips, bend straight down from your waist, touch your toes, fold into a sitting position, extend your arms, rise up, and touch your toes again. I do about a dozen of each loosening-up exercise. After I have finished loosening up, I'm ready to start running.

Running

Running is the most important exercise a pitcher can do. Remember, your legs as well as your pitching arm must be in superb shape. Every day of the season when I'm not pitching I go to the left field corner and do between 15 and 20 *wind sprints* across the outfield. By wind sprints I don't mean jogging; I mean a full-speed-ahead run. Wind sprints build stamina as well as strength.

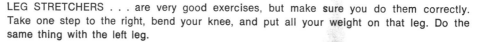

LEG STRETCHERS . . . are very good exercises, but make sure you do them correctly. Take one step to the right, bend your knee, and put all your weight on that leg. Do the same thing with the left leg.

Isometric Exercises

Isometric exercises pit one muscle against another and develop great body tone. I use isometrics to keep my wrists, forearms, shoulders, and back in shape. To tone my shoulders and forearms I stand in an open doorway, place the palms of my hands against the frame, and push outward as hard as I can. To exercise my back I reach up and grab the top of the door frame. Leaning forward, I pull back with my hands and try to hold my position with my back. To get my wrists and forearms in shape with isometrics I simply push the palms of my hands against each other as hard as I can. All of these exercises can be done at any place and time.

ISOMETRIC EXERCISES . . . can be done anywhere. They pit one muscle against another and build good body tone.

DURING THE SEASON—YOUR ARM

You check the runners and take the sign. You bring your right arm around smoothly, kick your leg high into the air, and start to come around with your arm. Everything is working smoothly, and you have good pitching rhythm. But at the last second, your success still depends on one thing — the physical ability of your arm to respond to your brain. The human arm is a magnificent collection of bone, muscle, and tissue; each part works together with the other parts in perfect harmony to perform assigned tasks. But the arm was never really intended to withstand the strain that pitching puts on it, so you must take proper care of it.

As with other simple machines, you must never make the arm work when it is cold. It must be warmed up carefully. When I'm scheduled to pitch, I begin the day by having the trainer give me a thorough rubdown to loosen the muscles in my arm. I also apply some deep heating lotion to my shoulder.

When I finally get out on the field, I begin warming up very slowly, first lobbing the ball a few feet to the catcher, then gradually increasing my distance until I'm the full 60 feet, 6 inches away from the plate. I continue lobbing the ball until my arm feels completely loose, and then I begin to throw a little harder. I work on my fast ball first, and once I'm throwing at full speed, I throw the fast ball for five minutes. Next I throw the curve for five minutes; then sliders for five minutes. Finally I throw three or four minutes of change-ups. I won't stop working on a pitch until I'm satisfied that it is going where I want it to go and doing what I think it should. My last ten pitches will be the entire repertoire: fast balls, curves, sliders, and change-ups. Then I put on my nylon jacket and wait until it is time for me to take the mound.

You might find that you can loosen up your arm in less time than it takes me to warm up. Most relief pitchers can get totally prepared in three or four minutes. Experiment until you discover what makes you feel most comfortable. You will know you haven't spent enough time warming up if your arm still feels tight when you have finished.

When I go out to pitch, I warm up with a series of pitches to get the feel of the mound.

My body is usually very stiff the day after I pitch, so I rest it completely. The only thing I do the day after pitching is to run in the outfield. I don't even touch a baseball. The following day I throw very easily for about 15 minutes. I won't really stretch the arm out, but I think you should throw every second day to maintain your control. I rest my arm completely again on the third day, and on the fourth day I start the rotation all over again. By taking your time and warming up correctly you save a great deal of wear and tear on your arm.

Taking Care of a Good Arm

There is no doubt that most pitchers have to be more careful with their arms than other players do. Not that they're any better or any worse players; it is just that they are more fragile. Decide what kind of exercise and how much pitching is right for you and stick to it. There is one thing I can universally recommend, though, and that is always to wear a jacket on the bases and in the dugout. It is important to keep your body temperature stable at all times when you're pitching, and a good jacket helps you to do so. The arm stiffens up easily when it cools down, so keep it covered to keep it loose.

Some pitchers like to soak their pitching arm in warm water or ice after they pitch.

I think that in most cases this is more of a mental comfort than anything else. The first person I ever heard of who soaked his arm after a game was Sandy Koufax, and he did it because he had such bad circulation. But after he started soaking his arm, almost all the other Dodger pitchers followed suit. A not-so-amazing thing happened, though, to all the pitchers who soaked their arms: the good ones remained good, and the bad ones stayed bad. If you think that soaking your arm works for you, it probably does. I never soak my arm after I pitch. I just take a hot shower, get dressed, and go home.

But some of the strangest things do work; Nolan Ryan, for example, soaks his hands in pickle brine to keep the blisters down. And when I was playing winter ball in Puerto Rico, we had a pitcher who refused to eat meat on the day he pitched and always covered his arm with snake oil. He may not have been very good, but he certainly attracted a lot of attention—and a lot of flies.

Taking Care of a Bad Arm

If you take proper care of your arm, it will stay healthy. But if you pitch too much, you'll end up with a tired arm. And if you don't take proper care of it, you'll end up with a sore arm.

I've never had a sore arm because I've always babied my "business interest." I have, however, had a tired arm. I've averaged over 300 innings pitched a year for most of my major league career, and toward the end of any season I can feel the strain. You'll know you have a tired arm when it feels heavy and doesn't have the spring that it had in April. Rest is the best cure. When I have a tired arm, I cut out the 15-minute workouts between starts. Be careful of a tired arm; it easily can lead to a sore one.

A sore arm can end your pitching career. There is nothing worse that could happen to a pitcher than a sore arm. When you first notice your arm is a little bit tight and you have to throw a little differently, it's time to stop throwing and consult your coach or trainer. Tell him about the tightness and where the pain is centered. For sore arms resulting from strain, rest is the only cure. But some sore arms are caused by a muscle tear or ruptured vessel, and these need medical attention. If the soreness is very bad or if it persists after a rest, go to a doctor.

DURING THE GAME

One of baseball's great cliches is, "pitching takes a lot out of you." It does indeed, and the thing it takes most is body salt. When you perspire, you lose a great amount of salt, and this loss can only make you physically weaker. For that reason I'm a firm believer in salt tablets. I start every game I pitch by gulping down half a dozen salt tablets; then I take two or three more every inning. If you take salt tablets, be careful not to drink too much water with them, or you will get stomach cramps. Salt tablets can cause you to get nauseous if you are not used to them, so don't overdo using them at first. When I'm pitching, I also eat one or two chocolate bars during a game. Chocolate is mostly sugar, and sugar provides quick energy. It may not work for you, but it works for me.

As for pacing myself during a game, I don't. Pacing separates the pitchers from the throwers. A pitcher knows that he is in top shape and can throw his best stuff for nine innings. A thrower works as hard as he can for as long as he can, and when his stuff is gone, he's gone. If you're in the second inning and you're worried about saving something for the last inning, don't worry. And if you're throwing so hard that you're losing your stuff, you won't be around much longer anyway.

EATING PROPERLY

One area you should pace yourself in is eating. It is easy to pick up a little extra weight, and if your body isn't used to carrying it around, you'll end up exhausted on the mound. I recommend that you eat as much protein as possible, in season and out. During the season I eat two meat meals a day and drink a tremendous amount of milk and juices. You know what your metabolism requires in the way of food, but don't give yourself too much extra.

The only pills I take are salt tablets to replace the body salt I lose through perspiration. There has been a lot of discussion lately about "greenies," and "red ones," and so on. Never, never take a pill unless it has been specifically prescribed for you by a competent physician.

DURING THE OFF-SEASON

Pitching is my profession, and I work at it 365 days a year. If you're serious about being a pitcher, you will realize it's a year-round job. Most of your time during the season should be devoted to the improvement of skills; your time during the off-season should be spent maintaining top physical condition. I work out at least three times a week during the winter, and very often when I'm sitting in my apartment, I do isometrics or get down on the floor and do sit-ups. Exercise is second nature to me; I do it instinctively. Your winter program should be divided into three areas: running, exercises, and a small amount of weight lifting.

Running

When your legs go, can your career be far behind? I think I've stressed the importance of keeping your legs in shape, and the winter is a good time to do it. I try to run at least three days a week during the off-season. One of the ways I get my running in is by playing basketball. Many clubs don't want their athletes playing basketball, but I think that it is a great conditioner. A group of Cubs and ex-Cubs who stay in the Chicago area during the winter have formed a basketball team, and we play through most of December and January. I'm not very good at basketball, but I have played more than 70 games with the fabulous Harlem Globetrotters.

Exercises

I do the same isometrics and basic series of exercises during the off-season that I do during baseball season. I do these exercises about two or three times a week. Exercising keeps the body in tone and the muscles loose. If your muscles are tight when pre-season practice begins, you have a pretty good chance of pulling one.

Weights

I've never been much of a weight lifter. I wear weighted shoes when I walk and weighted boots when I hunt to strengthen my legs, but beyond that I stay away from weights. You build up bulk muscle by weight lifting, which is fine for a hitter but not for a pitcher. I also recommend that you don't do a lot of swimming, because it builds up the wrong muscles for a pitcher.

SKILL IMPROVEMENT EXERCISES

Now that I have discussed exercises designed to improve your condition, I want to mention the exercises that are designed to make you a better pitcher—to improve your skills. Some of these exercises I've already mentioned, but they're worth a little further explanation in terms of body development.

Throwing at a Target

Few young pitchers get enough time on the mound to develop their control fully, so you must work on control on your own time. Set up a target. It doesn't matter what type—a pair of badminton standards, an old tire, a box on a wall, anything you can aim at. After you have developed the ability to get the ball in the box almost every time, start aiming for the corners, high and low, inside and outside.

Following Through

If you have access to an axe, I recommend that you chop as much wood as possible. The action involved in wood chopping is quite similar to the pitching follow-through. Besides, chopping wood helps you to strengthen your shoulder and back muscles. Following through also can be practiced in front of a full-length mirror. Go through your windup, and when you finish, you should be staring straight at yourself, with your arm extended and your feet balanced. Check to see that you follow through the same way every time. If you don't have an axe or a full-length mirror, simply go through the motion over and over, concentrating on your follow-through. Check your feet continually to make sure that they are ending up in approximately the same spot every time.

Release

To strengthen your wrists and make sure you are coming over the top when you release the ball, I suggest that you get a five-pound sledgehammer and practice hitting nails into a board. Keep up the hitting for about 20 minutes at a time to get the most benefit out of this exercise. If you don't have a sledgehammer, take an ordinary sock and roll it tight so that its length is about the same as the width of your hand. Then wrap it with tape and start squeezing. Carry it with you constantly, and whenever you have a spare moment, take it out and squeeze. This exercise will help to strengthen your wrist.

Pepper

Pepper is the best game a pitcher can play to improve his skills. Get a partner and have him hold the bat. Pitch the ball to him, and when he hits it, pitch it back to him as fast as you can. Playing pepper will improve your reflexes, your follow-through, and your ability to pick up the ball off the bat.

Daily Practice Schedule

No one likes to work out every day; the fun of baseball is playing it. But make a daily schedule for yourself and stick to it. Once you make a habit of daily exercise, you won't need a schedule.

INJURIES

No matter how careful you are, chances are that at one point or another you will be injured. All injuries, regardless of their extent or location, should be reported to your coach and team doctor. When they are cared for improperly, little injuries have a tendency to become big ones. The best cure for most baseball injuries is keeping the injured area clean and resting your entire body.

glossary

Angle of delivery: The type of delivery a pitcher uses in his motion; full, three-quarters, sidearm, and underhand are the customary angles of delivery.

Artificial turf: A manmade substance used to replace grass.

Athletic supporter: A piece of protective equipment worn over the genitals to prevent strains.

Backstop: The area of the playing field that is directly behind home plate; a pitched ball will hit the backstop if the catcher does not catch or block it. A slang expression for a catcher.

Balk: An illegal move made by the pitcher with a runner or runners on base, entitling all runners to advance one base.

Barrel: The top, or thickest part, of a baseball bat.

Base hit: A slang term indicating a single. A two-base hit would be a double, and a three-base hit, a triple.

Beanball: A pitch deliberately thrown at a batter's head. This pitch is illegal, and it may lead to the suspension of a pitcher.

Blooper: A novelty pitch that is thrown very slowly in a high arc. Often it is thrown as high as 10 feet off the ground.

Box score: The statistical report of a completed baseball game.

Breaking pitch: A pitch other than a straight pitch; a pitch that curves.

Brush back pitch: A pitch thrown close to the batter's body to make him stand farther away from the plate. It is usually thrown when a batter is crowding the plate or standing very close to it.

Bullpen: The warm-up area designated for relief pitchers.

Catcher's box: The area in which the catcher must catch the ball. If he catches the ball outside this area, it is called a catcher's balk, and the batter is credited with a ball.

Catcher's signal: The hand code given to a pitcher by a catcher to indicate what he wants him to do with a specific pitch. He may call for a particular pitch (fast ball, curve, etc.) or a pitchout, pick-off, or any other maneuver.

Change-up: A pitch that is slower than a batter expects.

Cleats: The metal points on the bottom of baseball shoes to provide good traction. A slang term for baseball shoes.

Complete game: A game in which the home team and the visiting team get all their necessary turns at bat; a game in which the pitcher is not replaced.

Cup: A fiber glass or steel protector that fits inside an athletic supporter and provides protection for the crotch area.

Curve ball: A pitch thrown by a right-handed pitcher that curves away from a right-handed hitter or thrown by a left-handed pitcher that curves away from a left-handed hitter.

Cut off: To intercept a throw coming from one direction and throw it in another direction.

Cut-off man: See *relay man*.

Delivery: The motion that the pitcher uses to throw the ball.

Dead ball: A ball out of play because of a legally created temporary suspension of play.

Doubleheader: Two regularly scheduled games played in succession.

Double play: A play by the defense in which two offensive players are put out as the result of a continuous action.

Double pumping: A type of pitching motion in which the pitcher brings his arms above his head twice before delivering the ball. It is used to throw off a batter's timing and to add power to the pitch.

Dugout: That area of the field in which players stay during a game when they are not involved in play on the field.

Earned run: A run for which a pitcher shall be held accountable; a run scored not as a result of an error.

Earned run average: A statistic computed by multiplying by nine the number of earned runs a pitcher has given up and then dividing by the total number of innings he has pitched. It is used to measure a pitcher's effectiveness.

Error: A misplay that enables a runner to reach base or to advance to another base on a ball that is usually playable.

Fair ball: A ball that is hit within the boundaries of the playing field.

Fast ball: A straight pitch thrown as hard as the pitcher can deliver it.

Fielder's choice: A situation in which a fielder handles a grounder and, instead of throwing to first to put out the runner, throws to another base in order to put out a runner on another base.

Fielding the position: The job of the pitcher after he delivers the ball. He must perform the job of an infielder if a ball is hit in his area.

Fireman: A slang term for a relief pitcher.

Flaps: Catcher's signals given by waving the entire hand rather than a specific number of fingers.

Fly: A ball hit to the outfield in an arc.

Follow-through: The motion of a pitcher after he has released the ball to prepare himself for fielding his position.

Force out: A play by which a runner is called out because the ball arrives at the base to which he must go before he gets there.

Force play: A situation in which a runner legally loses his right to occupy his base because a succeeding batter becomes a runner.

Fork ball: A pitch held between two fingers; this pitch tends to dip suddenly.

Foul ball: A ball that lands outside the boundary lines of the playing field without being touched by a fielder or fan.

Foul tip: A ball that is batted directly into the catcher's hands and is legally caught; a foul tip is considered a strike.

Full windup: The pitching motion used when there are no runners on base.

Grand slam: A home run hit while runners occupy all bases.

Ground rules: Those regulations relating to the specific ball park in which the game is to be played, designed to prevent any interference of normal play.

Hidden ball trick: A play in which a fielder holds the ball without the runner's knowledge; this play is designed to put a runner out.

Hit and run: A play in which the batter hits to a specific spot at the same time a base runner begins to run; the fielder will usually vacate the spot to play the runner, and the ball will go through for a hit.

Hit batsman: A legal batter who is struck with a pitched ball. He is entitled to take first base.

Illegal pitch: A throw that does not conform to the rules governing treatment of the baseball (a pitcher adds saliva or cuts the cover, for examples); a pitch delivered to the batter when the pitcher is not in contact with the pitching rubber.

Indicator: A sign that means another sign will follow.

Infield: That area of the playing field occupied by the pitcher, catcher, shortstop, and basemen.

Infielder: Anyone who plays in the infield, including the first, second, and third basemen, the shortstop, the pitcher, and the catcher.

Inning: A division of a baseball game in which both teams get one complete turn at bat. There are nine innings in a regulation game.

Intentional pass: Four balls thrown purposefully by the pitcher far enough away from the plate so that the batter cannot strike at them; the batter is awarded a walk.

Interference: A situation in which an offensive player obstructs, impedes, or confuses a fielder attempting to play a ball or a defensive player prevents a batter from hitting a pitch.

Isometrics: A system of conditioning exercises in which one muscle is pitted against another.

Jump: The lead a base runner takes off the base.

Knuckle ball: A pitch that is totally unpredictable; often called a butterfly.

Laces: The threads that hold a baseball together.

Letters: The name or nickname of a team, written across a player's uniform.

Lineup: The batting order of the nine players who start a game.

Long man: The relief pitcher who specializes in coming into the game in the early innings and attempting to finish the game.

Middle-inning pitcher: The relief pitcher who comes into the game and is expected to pitch two to four innings successfully.

Money pitch: A slang term for a pitcher's most dependable pitch.

Mud guards: Flat metal plates attached to the bottom of a player's cleats to prevent the accumulation of mud.

Novelty pitches: An unusual pitch. It may even be something a pitcher invents or a ball, such as the blooper or fork ball, which turns up every few years.

Opposite field: The area of the field to which a batter is not expected to be able to hit. For example, the opposite field for a right-handed hitter is right field; for a left-handed hitter, left field.

Outfield: That area composed of left field, right field, and center field.

Palm ball: A pitch delivered with the palm of the hand. This pitch acts much like a change-of-pace, but it drops at the last minute.

Passed ball: A pitch playable by the catcher that eludes him, thus allowing a runner or runners to advance.

Pepper game: A warm-up session in which a batter and at least one fielder stand at least ten feet apart; the fielder throws the ball, and the batter repeatedly hits it back to him.

Percentage baseball: A type of baseball strategy based on what usually has happened in similar situations.

Pick-off: An attempt to catch a base runner while he is standing off base by having the fielder tag him before he can return.

Pinch hitter: A batter who substitutes for the scheduled hitter.

Pinch runner: A base runner who substitutes for a player who already occupies a base.

Pitching chart: A pitch-by-pitch account of a game, which explains graphically where every pitch went, whether it was a ball or strike, what type of pitch it was, and, if hit, where it went. This chart helps pitchers to learn hitters' strengths and weaknesses.

Pitching rotation: The order in which a team's pitching staff starts ball games.

Pitching staff: The pitchers on a baseball team.

Pitchout: A pitch deliberately thrown wide of the plate. This ball usually is called by the catcher when he feels that a base runner will attempt to steal on a particular pitch.

Pop-up: A fly ball playable by an infielder.

Quick pitch: A ball delivered by the pitcher to the batter before he is ready; an illegal pitch.

Relay man: A player who intercepts a throw and throws it to another player in the original or a different direction.

Relief pitcher: A player who replaces a pitcher already in the game.

Resin bag: A porous cloth bag containing a substance that is applied to keep hands from sweating.

Run: A complete circuit of the bases; a score.

Run and hit: A play in which the base runner attempts to advance as the pitch is delivered in order to make a fielder vacate a spot for the hitter.

Rundown: A play involving at least two fielders that is initiated when a base runner is caught between bases and is attempting to reach base safely.

Sacrifice: A bunt the purpose of which is to advance a man already on base; a fly that is playable by an outfielder enables a man on third to tag up and score.

Safety squeeze: A bunt play in which a runner on third base waits to see if the batter is successful in laying down the bunt before breaking for the plate.

Save: The statistic credited to a relief pitcher who enters the game with his team in the lead and maintains that lead; the scoring term used to designate the relief pitcher who pitched most effectively if more than one pitcher maintained the lead.

Screwball: A pitch that when thrown by a right-handed pitcher, breaks in on a right-handed hitter; when thrown by a left-handed pitcher, it breaks in on a left-handed hitter.

Semiintentional pass: Pitching very carefully to a certain hitter in a situation in which it would not hurt to walk him; giving a batter nothing good to swing at.

Set position: The middle part of the stretch motion, when a pitcher halts.

Short man: A relief pitcher expected to pitch only briefly.

Shutout: A game in which one team is held scoreless by the opposition.

Sidearm: A pitching motion in which the ball is delivered from approximately a nine o'clock position.

Signal: A manual code intended to initiate a specific play.

Sinker: A pitch that drops down as it crosses the plate.

Slide: A means of reaching a base by propelling the body across the ground.

Slider: A curve ball that does not drop.

Spitball: A pitch to which saliva is added to make the ball move in various directions; an illegal pitch.

Spot starter: A starting pitcher not included in the regular rotation.

Starting pitcher: The pitcher named in the lineup to begin the game.

Steal: The action of a runner who attempts to advance to the next base without being forced, without the ball's being hit, and without being awarded the base by an umpire. He attempts to move to that base while the ball is being pitched.

Stepping in the bucket: A slang term indicating that a batter is stepping away from home plate with his front foot as the ball is pitched rather than stepping in the direction of the pitch, as he should.

Stepping off: A movement in which the pitcher moves off the pitcher's mound.

Stepping out: A movement in which the batter steps out of the batter's box.

Stopper: A slang term meaning the best pitcher on a pitching staff.

Stretch position: The motion a pitcher uses with men on base. It is a two-part motion interrupted by a pause in the middle. This halt prevents base runners from running to the next base during the motion.

Strike: A ball pitched within the strike zone; a pitch at which the batter swings and misses; a foul ball not caught by a fielder.

Strikeout: A situation in which a batter is retired on three strikes.

Strike zone: That area over the plate between the top of the batter's knees and his shoulders.

Submarine: A type of delivery in which the ball is thrown almost underhand, at approximately a six o'clock position.

Suicide squeeze: A bunt play in which a runner on third base starts to come home as the ball is pitched. If the batter is successful in bunting the ball, he will usually be safe; otherwise he probably will be tagged out by the catcher.

Suspended game: A game in which the trailing team has not batted at least five times; the game must be resumed at the point of interruption.

Switch hitter: A player who is capable of batting effectively both left-handed and right-handed.

Tagging up: Attempting to advance to another base after a ball has been caught.

Tag play: A situation in which a runner has not been forced to vacate his base; in order to be called out he must be touched between bases by the fielder holding the ball.

Take: To let a pitch go by without swinging.

Takeout: To slide into a fielder in order to keep him from throwing the ball.

Texas leaguer: A pop fly that falls between the infielders and the outfielders.

Three-quarters overhand: A type of pitching motion in which the pitcher's arm comes over his shoulder at approximately a ten o'clock position.

Time: Temporary suspension of play.

Toe plate: A piece of equipment the pitcher wears on the front of his spikes to prevent wear.

Umpire: A judge designated to make sure that a game is conducted according to standard league rules. An umpire calls balls, strikes, outs, fair and foul balls, and any penalties that may occur.

Waste pitch: A pitch intentionally thrown far enough outside the strike zone so that the batter can't hit it.

Wild pitch: A throw that is so wild it is unplayable by the catcher.

Win: A game in which a pitcher has pitched more than five innings and either completes the game or leaves the game with his team leading; his team must maintain that lead.

Wind sprints: Running exercises that keep legs in condition; usually a series of 25- to 100-yard dashes at full speed.

index